THEN AND THERE SERIES
GENERAL EDITOR
MARJORIE REEVES

Mary Queen of Scots and the Scottish Reformation

WILLIAM K RITCHIE

Illustrated from contemporary sources

LONGMAN

LONGMAN GROUP LIMITED
*Longman House, Burnt Mill, Harlow, Essex CM20, 2JE, England
and Associated Companies throughout the World.*

First published 1979
Second impression 1983
ISBN 0 582 21725 3

Printed in Hong Kong
by Commonwealth Printing Press Ltd.

To James Miller

Contents

To the Reader

This book is about one of the most famous women who ever lived. Books, plays, films, an opera and a ballet have all been written about her. Ask almost any group of people and you can be sure that one of them has heard about Mary Queen of Scots. This book will perhaps help you to understand why.

But this book is not just about a famous queen. It tells you also about the time in which she lived, especially about the great changes in religion that were taking place which still affect the lives of people in Scotland to this day.

Words printed in *italics* in the text are explained in the Glossary on page 92.

1   A Child Queen

The picture on the next page is of Linlithgow Palace in Scotland. Today it is a roofless ruin, but hundreds of years ago kings and queens lived here. The rooms and passages echoed with the sound of music and laughter. There was always bustle and activity. It would have been like that when the court was here early in December 1542. Imagine that you had been there. On 8 December you might have been pushed aside as *courtiers* and servants rushed about passing on the exciting news. The Queen had just had a baby! A little girl!

You would have quickly seen that many were sorry the baby was not a boy. The King and Queen had no other children, so this little girl would be the next ruler of Scotland. People at this time were used to being ruled by men and did not like the idea of a woman ruling them. Within a few days the baby was baptised in the nearby church of St Michael. She was called Mary, like her mother.

The baby's father was not at the christening. King James V was lying very ill at Falkland Palace in Fife. People said that he had lost the will to live. Recently he had quarrelled with the King of England, and when his army crossed the Border into England it was scattered in a battle fought at Solway Moss near Carlisle. Some of his best soldiers were killed and many of his nobles were taken prisoner. When the messenger told him that the Queen had given birth to a daughter instead of a son, it is said that he groaned and said: 'Alas! it came with a lass and it will pass with a lass.' He was thinking of how his family, the Stewarts, had come to rule Scotland through a 'lass', Marjorie, daughter of King Robert the Bruce.

Now, he was afraid, they would stop ruling Scotland with a 'lass', his little daughter, Mary. On 14 December 1542 James V died, leaving Mary to become Queen of Scots when she was less than a week old.

THE ROUGH WOOING

With a baby as queen, the country would have to be ruled by a *regent*. Two men claimed this right: *Cardinal* David Beaton and James Hamilton, Earl of Arran. Beaton said that he should look after the country for the baby Queen because he

*Cardinal Beaton,
who tried and failed
to keep up the
Auld Alliance with France*

had been her father's chief adviser. The Earl of Arran, however, said that he had a better right because, as you can see from the family tree over the page, he was related to the royal family.

Opposite: *Linlithgow Palace, where Mary Queen of Scots was born, with St Michael's Church where she was christened, standing beside it*

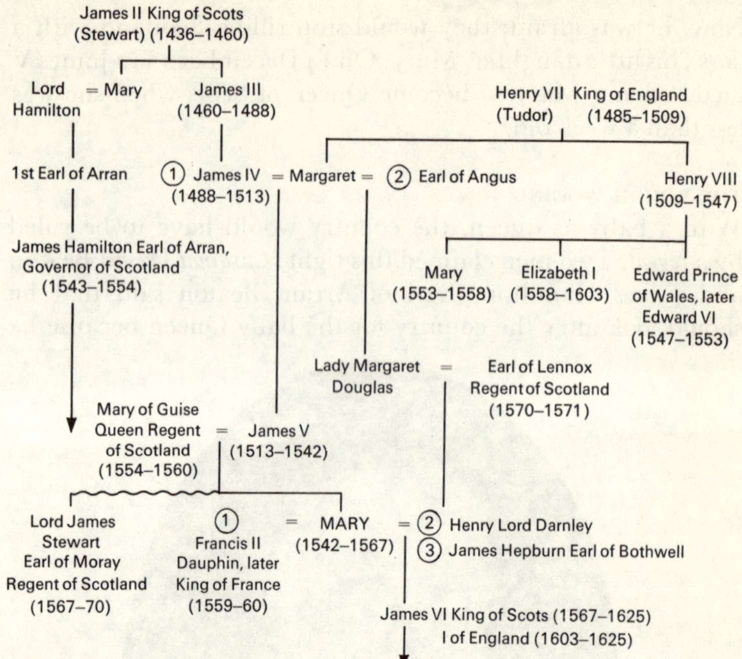

This family-tree shows how many of the people in this book were related

People outside Scotland were also very interested in who should govern Scotland. Just like boys and girls playing on a see-saw, the countries of Europe were all grouped behind one or other of the two most powerful rulers of the time, the King of France and the Emperor, who ruled not only the Empire in Germany but also Spain and the Low Countries. As an old rival of France, the King of England sided with the Emperor; and since England was the 'auld enemy' of Scotland, the Scots kept up their 'Auld *Alliance*' with France. Each side was always afraid that the other would become too powerful and so upset the see-saw, that is, the balance of power. Now that Scotland was without a strong ruler the balance of power was upset: England and the Emperor were more powerful than France alone. The French therefore wanted to hold on to Scotland as an ally, and the English wanted to take Scotland away from France. So you can see why both sides took a great interest in what happened in Scotland.

The ruler of England was King Henry VIII. As you can see from the family tree on page 8, he was closely related to the Scottish royal family. James V was his nephew, but the two Kings had never been friends and their quarrelling had led to the recent war. Now that James was dead, Henry saw his chance to bring Scotland under his control and stop the French from using Scotland to invade England.

Henry knew it would not be easy. The little Queen's mother, Mary of Guise, was French and wanted to keep up the Auld Alliance. So did Cardinal Beaton. Henry had therefore to stop Beaton from being made regent and get Arran appointed instead, because Arran wanted an alliance with England. Henry hoped that he could make Arran agree to a marriage of the little Queen of Scots to his son, Edward, the young Prince of Wales, so uniting the two countries. But how was Henry to do all this?

Henry knew that the Scottish nobles whom the English had captured at Solway Moss longed to go home. So he said that they could return if they first promised that they would do all they could to help him take over Scotland. He invited them to spend Christmas with him and presented each of them with a golden chain and enough horses and money for their journey. Henry's plan worked. When they got back to Scotland these 'assured lords', as they were called, managed to get the Earl of Arran made Governor. They also made sure that *ambassadors* were appointed to arrange for Prince Edward to marry Queen Mary.

Then things began to go wrong for King Henry. Seeing through Henry's schemes, Cardinal Beaton and Mary of Guise, with help from France, were able to win over the Earl of Arran to their side. He put some of the 'assured lords' in prison. He sent the baby Queen to Stirling Castle for safe keeping in case Henry tried to kidnap her. A treaty arranging for Queen Mary to marry Prince Edward was signed at Henry's palace at Greenwich in July 1543. But when Henry demanded that the Scottish Queen should be brought up in England, Arran cancelled the treaty.

Henry VIII was not used to his plans being upset like this. Having failed to persuade the Scots to let their Queen marry his son, he decided to use force. In May 1544 he ordered one of his best generals, the Earl of Hertford, to invade Scotland with an army of 10,000 men by land and sea. These were Hertford's orders:

> Put all to fire and sword, burn Edinburgh, beat down the castle, *sack* Holyroodhouse and as many towns and villages as you can; sack Leith, putting man, woman and child to sword without exception where any resist you.

Hertford faithfully carried out these instructions. For the rest of that year the English army went about the Scottish Border, burning down castles and towns and stealing cattle and sheep. Nobody seemed able to stop them.

Then, in February 1545, the Scots won a victory over their enemy. The Earl of Douglas, head of the powerful Douglas family, and one of Henry's 'assured lords', changed sides and fought against the English because they had destroyed his family tomb in Melrose Abbey. The Scots came upon the English encamped on a moor to the north of Ancrum, near Jedburgh. Outnumbered five to one, the Scots at first were unwilling to fight, but they defeated the English by a trick. While most of the Scots dismounted and hid behind a hill, the camp-followers got on to the horses and suddenly appeared on still higher ground. This made the English think that the Scots were in full retreat. So they decided to give chase. Breathless they arrived at the top of the hill only to find, to their surprise, the Scottish soldiers drawn up on foot on the other side armed with their long spears. The English horsemen charged, but the Scottish spearmen held firm and threw them back. Then, as a *chronicler* of the time tells us, 'they rushed them so rudely to the earth, that the noise was like the roaring of the sea'. Blinded by the light of the setting sun and by smoke from their own *arquebuses*, the English turned and fled. About

800 Englishmen were killed and a thousand taken prisoner. Scottish losses were small. So, after suffering so many defeats the Scots took heart from their victory at Ancrum Moor. When French help came they were able to clear the English from all the Border country.

The same chronicler who told us about the battle at Ancrum Moor also tells us that when Henry VIII heard about it he 'burned like fire and was *boldened* with *ire* so that for a long space no man *durst* speak to him'. So the Earl of Hertford was sent north again with an army to invade Scotland. He crossed the Tweed early in September 1545, choosing the time of year which would cause people the most hardship: harvest was late, and so the crops in the most fertile parts of Scotland were burned down. Towns and villages of the Borders were turned into black and smouldering ruins. So were the rich Border abbeys, Kelso, Jedburgh, Dryburgh and Melrose: all were cruelly plundered and destroyed. Proudly Hertford reported that so much damage had not been done in Scotland for the last hundred years.

In this way Henry VIII tried to make the Scots agree to the marriage of his son to their Queen. He did not succeed. An old-fashioned word for trying to persuade a woman to marry a man is 'wooing'. So, the Scots spoke about Henry's bullying methods to win over their country as 'the Rough Wooing'.

MURDER AT ST ANDREWS

The English King now tried another way to gain the upper hand in Scotland, by murdering his chief enemy there, Cardinal Beaton. As long as he was alive Scotland would be loyal to France. But Beaton had many enemies in Scotland. Some hated him because they thought Scotland should become friendly with England. Others were simply jealous of his great power and despised him for his coarse living. In 1544 some plotters let Henry know that they would murder Beaton if he paid them and Henry secretly told them to go ahead with their plans. Their leader was Norman Leslie, sheriff of Fife

arx episcopi
collegium div Salvatoris
ædes franciscanorum
ecclesia parochialis sancti Trinitatis
ædes dominicanorum
divæ Mariæ
collegium divi Leonardi

and son of the Earl of Rothes. He wanted revenge on the Cardinal for cheating him out of some land.

In May 1546 Cardinal Beaton was living in his castle at St Andrews, where he slept soundly at nights because he knew that his castle was defended on three sides by the North Sea and that the walls were kept in good repair. Early on the morning of Saturday 29 May the guards lowered the drawbridge as usual, to let in workmen who were repairing the walls. But amongst them that day were Norman Leslie and his friends. While one took up the porter's attention, the others slipped past unseen, with their weapons. Suddenly the porter saw what was happening. But before he could raise the alarm he was quickly silenced, and the plotters threw his body into the moat. In no time at all they had taken control of the castle hardly making a sound.

Cardinal Beaton, meanwhile, had woken up and sensed what was happening. Finding the *postern gate* locked, he rushed back to his room and frantically blocked up the door with furniture. The plotters began to burn down the door. Beaton unlocked it. There they found him, cowering in a chair. 'I am a priest! I am a priest!' he cried, begging for mercy. 'Ye will not slay me!' But they did, striking him with their swords time and time again.

Outside, the tolling of church bells sounded the alarm. The townsfolk came running to help. But it was too late. There on the castle walls they saw a grisly sight: dangling upside down by an arm and leg was the hacked and bleeding body of Cardinal Beaton.

THE SIEGE OF ST ANDREWS CASTLE
Henry VIII could smile with satisfaction now that Beaton was dead. Without him the Earl of Arran must surely make an alliance with England. But the Queen Mother, Mary of Guise, was more determined than ever to keep up the alliance with

Opposite: *A sketch of St Andrews in the sixteenth century. See if you can pick out the main streets, the town walls, the harbour, the cathedral beside the harbour, St Salvator's College with its tall tower (top left) and the castle (top centre)*

France. She persuaded the Governor to try to bring Beaton's murderers to justice. But the murderers locked themselves in Beaton's castle and refused to come out. With all the food and ammunition which the Cardinal had stored away in the castle they got ready to resist a long siege.

Because the murderers were holding his son *hostage* in the castle, the Governor did not try very hard to capture it. He hoped the defenders would run short of food and be starved into surrender. Both sides were playing for time. Every day they kept on looking out for help to come by sea: the besiegers looked for a fleet from France, the defenders of the castle looked for a fleet from England. At last, early in July 1547, the sails of a great fleet could be seen on the horizon. Whose were they, French or English? A cheer went up from the besiegers. The flags showed that the ships were French, sixteen galleys sent by the King of France to preserve the Auld Alliance.

The French landed. Just after daybreak one morning they opened fire with their heavy guns. The *bombardment* lasted six hours. One of the castle towers was shot away and the whole of the south wall became a pile of stones. Still the defenders held out. Then, just as the French were ready to take the castle by storm a white flag appeared and one of the defenders came out to ask for a cease-fire. After fourteen months the siege was over. With booty worth £100,000 and the defenders of the castle as prisoners of the French king, the French galleys sailed away. Cardinal Beaton's death had been avenged and once again English plans for Scotland had been foiled.

THE BATTLE OF PINKIE

Henry VIII died in January 1547 and his son became king as Edward VI. But he was only a boy of nine, so his uncle, the Earl of Hertford, now promoted to be Duke of Somerset, ruled the country as Lord Protector. Somerset was just as determined as Henry to conquer Scotland and so at the end of August 'the Rough Wooing' began again. While a fleet of sixty supply ships sailed up the coast, Somerset crossed the Border at the head of 16,000 men and marched on Edinburgh.

The Scottish leaders gathered an army of 20,000 to meet the invaders. Most of them were foot soldiers, but there were 1,500 light cavalry from the Borders. From the accounts kept by the *Lord Treasurer* we can tell that the Scots' army was well armed. Officers and men were dressed in white leather armour. Each soldier was supplied with a steel helmet, a sword, a dagger and a *pike* six metres long. There were plenty of cannon. From the distance an Englishman said that the Scottish army looked like 'great ridges of ripe barley'.

To halt the English march on Edinburgh, the Scots took up a good position to the east of the town, on a stretch of level ground on the left bank of the river Esk near Musselburgh. Their left flank was protected by the Firth of Forth, their centre by the steep bank of the river, and their right flank by

English soldiers with their long pikes. What shows that these pikemen were used to riding on horseback?

a marsh. The English army, meanwhile, set up its camp on the other side of the Esk at Prestonpans. From here Somerset spread out his men for about 2.3 kilometres as far as Falside Hill to the south-west. Look carefully at the positions of the two armies on the map below.

The English army was smaller than the Scottish army, but its leaders and men had more experience and were better disciplined. Most of them were foot soldiers armed with pikes, but there were also archers and *hagbutters*. Somerset however had decided to rely mainly on his 4,000 heavy cavalry including about 200 Spaniards who were trained to shoot arquebuses as they rode. He planned to used his *cavalry* with his artillery: to keep the Scottish pikemen pinned down with swift cavalry charges and then blast them with heavy cannon-fire.

This plan shows the positions of the English and Scottish armies before the Battle of Pinkie

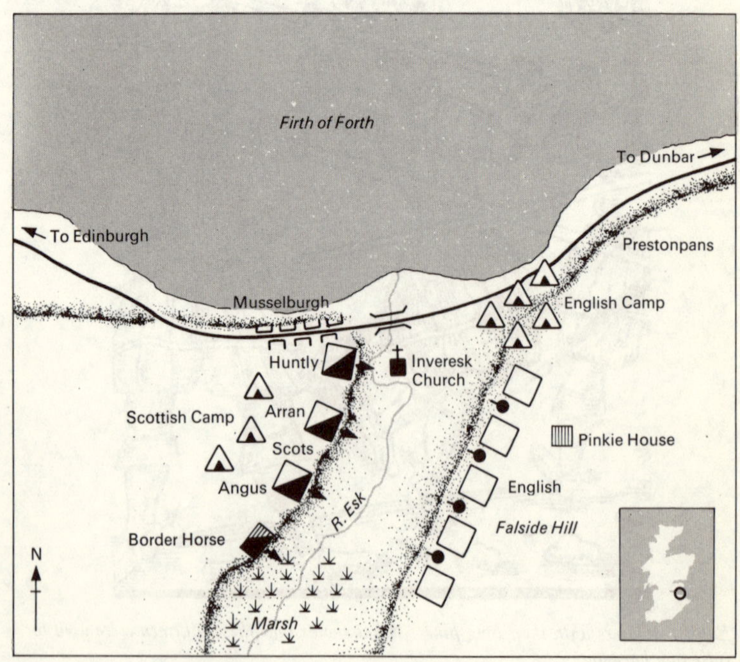

The Scots looked stronger than they really were. The Earl of Arran was an uninspiring leader and many of the other nobles were undependable: some of them had in the past fought for the English, and might change sides again. Most of the soldiers had never fought together before. The Border horse-troopers from the start showed how badly disciplined they were: they broke ranks and were cut to pieces by the English heavy cavalry. So the Scots lost most of their cavalry before the battle had even started.

Fighting started early on 10 September when Somerset moved his men down from Falside Hill to place guns near Inveresk church, on a little hill overlooking the Scottish lines. From here they would be able to fire straight on to the Scottish centre. Already the English ships were within firing distance of the Scottish left wing. So now he would be able to throw the whole of the Scottish army into confusion. But the Earl of Arran thought that the English army was getting ready to withdraw. So, to cut them off, he ordered his right wing to advance. As a result of a misunderstanding, however, the Scottish left wing also advanced, crossed the bridge over the Esk and began to turn southwards. The two wings of the Scottish army were therefore steadily marching into each other. What made matters worse for the Scots, gunfire from the English ships terrified the Highlanders on the left wing who were not used to the noise.

Somerset now saw that the Scots had thrown away the advantage of their strong position. Smartly he ordered his men to form up and face the enemy: pikemen in the centre, flanked by archers and hagbutters with cannon in the spaces between, and with cavalry on each wing of the whole army – light cavalry on the right, heavy cavalry on the left.

On the word of command the English heavy cavalry now charged the Scottish right wing. To meet this tremendous attack the Scots formed their usual 'schiltron', or hedgehog formation, with their pikes facing outwards. Just imagine what it must have been like to be one of these English cavalrymen charging down on this mass of steel bristles. You would be

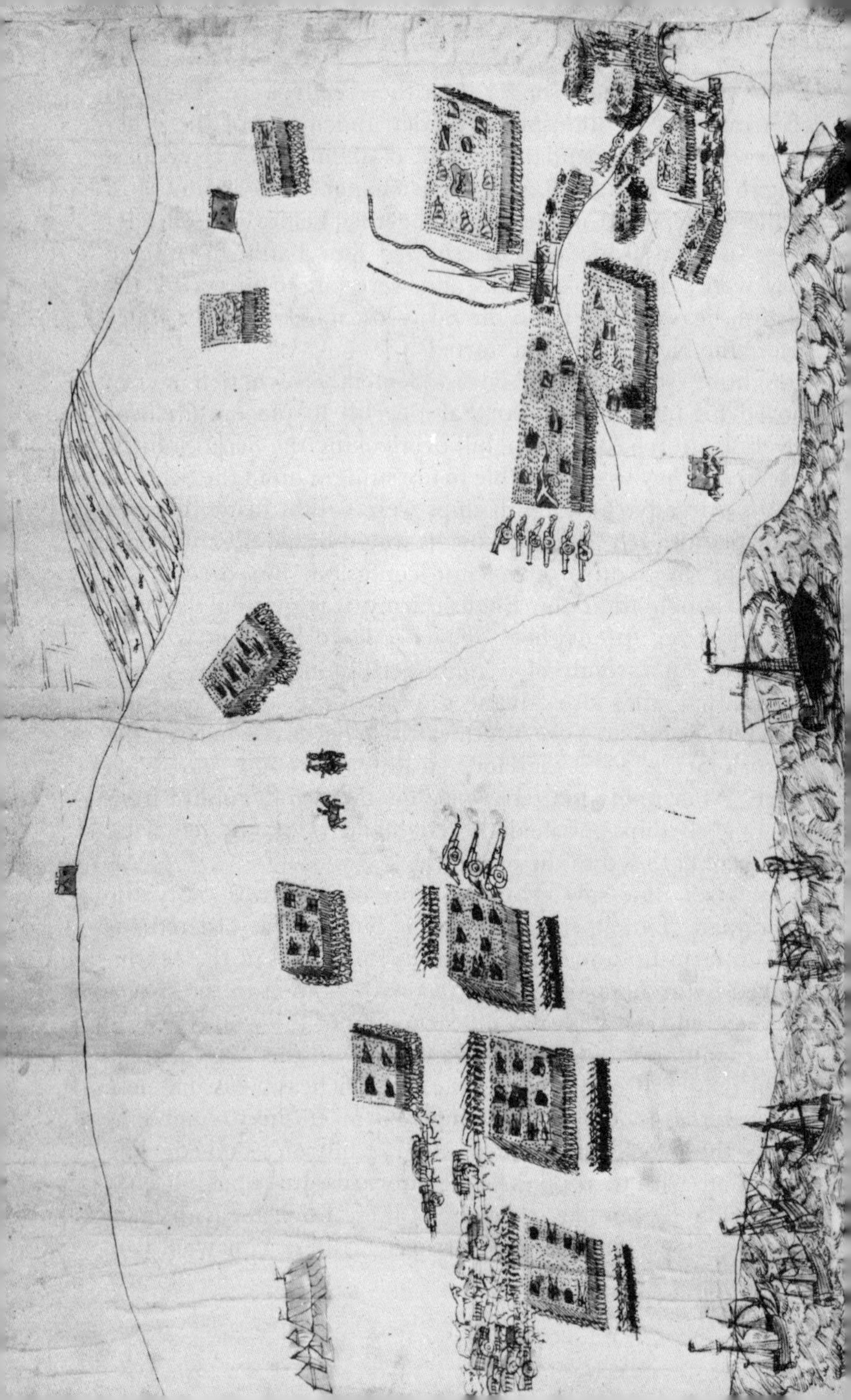

clad in armour from head to foot and your horse protected with a thick linen cover, but still…the fierce yells would grow louder as the Scots poised their pikes to hold you back. … Imagine the thunder of hooves, the jangle of harness, and then the sudden crack of splintering pikes and lances as they came together. Think of the scowls, the curses, the shouts, the gasps, the groans, the cries of pain from the men, and the horrible neighing of the horses as they reared and thudded to the ground or charged about riderless among the fallen and into the oncoming waves of other horsemen surging into the attack. The slaughter was terrible. Heavy-armoured knights, wallowing helplessly on the ground, were savagely finished off by the Scottish pikemen with their daggers. Two hundred horsemen fell in that first wave alone. Three hundred more were killed in later attacks until they finally retreated uphill.

But the English cavalry returned. Now it was the turn of the gunners to play their part in the battle too. Red-hot shot poured out of barrels of the cannon and scattered the tight-knit ranks of the Scottish spearmen. All the time the English archers were raining down arrows, and the mounted Spanish hagbutters dashed in to fire off shot into the faces of the helpless Scots.

Soon it was all over. The Scottish army collapsed. The Earl of Arran turned and fled. By one o'clock the Scots were in full flight, scattered in all directions. Relentlessly the English troopers followed, slashing at the helpless fugitives. The river Esk ran with blood. The whole area was strewn with corpses 'as cattle in a well-stocked pasture field'. Between 8,000 and 14,000 Scots were killed and over 1,000 taken prisoner in the battle of Pinkie (or Falside Hill as it is sometimes called). It was almost as terrible as the battle of Flodden, fought almost exactly thirty-four years before.

Meanwhile where had little Queen Mary been during these years of looting, murder and fighting? Most of the time she had been safe in the care of her mother and nurses at Stirling Castle. During the time of the battle of Pinkie, however, she had been taken even further out of harm's way to the *priory* of Inchmahome on a tiny island in the middle of the Lake of Menteith. After the battle of Pinkie Somerset had gone home. But supposing he returned and tried to capture her, would she be safe even here?

Mary of Guise, her mother, thought that nowhere in Scotland was safe. So she asked the French king to send more help to Scotland and to arrange for Mary to be sent to France for safety.

French help was needed more than ever now because in the spring of 1548 English armies were once again in Scotland, going out on raids from their base at Haddington. In the middle of June a French army landed at Leith and joined the Scots in besieging Haddington. In a *nunnery* nearby Scots and French leaders signed a very important treaty. The French promised to go on defending Scotland as if it was a part of their own country and Mary was to be sent to France and later marry the *dauphin*, the French King's son.

The ships that had brought the French troops now sailed round the north of Scotland to the Firth of Clyde. There at Dumbarton Queen Mary was safely taken on board. In this power game between France and England, France had won the first round. But would the French be able to hold on to Scotland? No one could tell in 1548.

2 *A French Upbringing*

Although no doubt sad to leave her mother, Mary was probably
also very excited at going away on such a long journey. There
would be plenty of things to take up her attention. Besides, she
had lots of lords and ladies to look after her and four little
girls about her own age of six to keep her company. These
were her special friends, her 'Four Maries', Mary Beaton,
Mary Seton, Mary Fleming and Mary Livingston. So she
would not be lonely.

Mary's ships sailed to France round the west coast of
Ireland. This was to miss any English ships that might try to
capture her. We can learn about Mary's voyage to France
from letters that were written to her mother by Monsieur de
Brézé, a Frenchman who had been chosen to look after her.
Off Land's End he reported,

> When the sea was wondrously wild with the biggest waves
> I ever saw in my life, to our great horror and dismay the
> rudder of our galley was smashed. But still our Lord was
> pleased to *intervene* so that we replaced the rudder at once,
> in spite of the heavy sea that was running. The queen has
> been less ill upon the sea than any of our company, so that
> she made fun of those that were.

The Queen Mother was probably relieved when she read at
last: 'We landed here at St Pol de Léon on the 15th of this
month of August, after a stormy passage of eighteen days on
the sea.' Since St Pol de Léon is inland it was probably the
little port of Roscoff where Mary actually landed in France. 21

A galley like this took Mary to France. Note the rows of oars and the flags showing the silver lilies of the French king

AT THE COURT OF THE KING OF FRANCE

Mary spent the next thirteen years in France. Later when she looked back she might have thought them the happiest time in her life. Everywhere she was treated with the greatest respect and kindness. Her French grandmother, Duchess Antoinette of Guise, looked after her at first. She was a stern but kind old lady, well known for her common sense and dry humour. She took Mary to meet the French King Henry II and he liked the child at once. He was a tall, dark man who rarely smiled but who got on well with children. He had three of his own then, Francis the Dauphin, aged five, and two little girls, Elisabeth and Claude. The Queen of France, Catherine, was also pleased with Mary and remarked, 'Our little Scottish queen has but to smile to turn all French heads.'

Mary was brought up at court with the royal children. At

the French court people did everything to make life pleasant
and beautiful. Take the royal castles, for instance: they look
as if they had been taken out of a book of children's fairy tales.
Many of them stood in the valley of the river Loire, one of the
most beautiful parts of France. Although we call them *châteaux*
these were not castles built to stand up to attacks and long
sieges, but royal hunting-lodges. Here the king and his friends
used to stay for months at a time and go out hunting in the
woods round about for wild boar, wolves and deer. Then they
would move on to another royal castle.

Kings at this time were always on the move. They had no
fixed capital city where they lived most of the time but travelled
about their country seeing that it was properly governed.

Use this map to find many of the places mentioned in this book

Wherever they went, all their government officials went too, along with their families and servants. You might have seen as many as 18,000 people travelling about France together: ladies and gentlemen riding on horseback, servants sitting on top of heavy wagons with all their belongings – not only clothes, but bedding, furniture and even pots and pans as well!

The royal household accounts show us how often the French court moved about. From January to April 1550, for example, Mary and the royal children were living at St Germain, near Paris; they spent a short time nearby at Fontainebleau until 1 May; returned to St Germain for the summer and moved on to three other palaces between October and the end of the year.

The insides of these castles and palaces were even more splendid than the outsides. As a visitor, you would have marvelled at the polished floors of wood or marble, the walls covered with coloured *frescoes* and wooden panelling painted. with gold, and the ceilings decorated with elaborate figures made out of plaster. But you would not have found them very comfortable places in which to live. There were very few chairs and not much other furniture either, except for a few tables and cabinets. And there were no toilets. Members of the royal family had *commodes*, padded in velvet and covered with a *canopy* like a tent, but many lords and ladies simply relieved themselves where they could, in a corner of a room perhaps or in the fireplace. So, to kill unpleasant smells the floors were scattered with sweet-smelling herbs, and courtiers sniffed at little *pomanders* that they carried about with them all the time.

Everything at the French court was done for show and not for comfort. You can also see this in the clothes the courtiers wore. Everybody seemed to be trying to dress more splendidly than anyone else. Since Mary was a queen she had always to look her very best. From her treasurer's accounts we can tell that she had dresses made of violet, crimson and yellow velvet, white satin and gold *damask*, with linings made of white silk and satin, and muffs of velvet trimmed with *sable*. In 1551

A banquet scene of the time looked like this. What are the dogs in the foreground doing?

she had sixteen such dresses made for her, with more than ten pairs of shoes to match. To go with her dresses she had many pairs of gloves, fans, chains and belts. Like the combs, brushes and mirrors she used, many of them were decorated with gold and jewels. Mary loved jewels so much that before she left France she needed three large chests to hold them all.

Mary was surrounded by servants. About 150 were needed to look after the royal children alone. These included 28 menservants, 22 nursemaids, 4 masters of the wardrobe, 5 doctors, 3 *apothecaries* and 4 barbers, but only 2 laundresses and 1 water-carrier, so you can judge for yourself how clean the royal nursery was!

Queen Catherine had introduced many new kinds of Italian food into France. There were different sorts of cheese and fruit, strange new vegetables and sausages. How would you have liked to sample any of these dishes: salted pork tongues cooked in wine, spit-roasted skylarks, pears wrapped in marzipan, or stuffed fat geese covered with almonds and served with sugar, cheese and cinnamon? Mary would have taken dishes like these at the magnificent *banquets* prepared for the royal family. Food was not served in our way. Even the grandest lords and ladies cut up their meat and ate it with their fingers and then wiped their hands on their clothes or on the tablecloth.

It must have cost a fortune to run the royal household even for food alone. In 1554 Mary was given a separate household of her own. As a result her governess was for ever writing to Mary of Guise to ask for more money. In one year Mary's expenses amounted to 58,607 *livres* and her income came to only 58,000 livres. But kings and nobles were always in debt. At the end of his reign Henry II of France had run up a debt of 40 million livres.

Much money was spent on entertainment. Mary had horses of her own, and enjoyed riding and hunting. She also went in for archery and tennis, which was then a fairly new sport, and quite different from the game played nowadays at Wimbledon. An older form of outdoor entertainment was the tournament, which Mary loved to watch with other members of the court. Indoor games included cards, chess and *backgammon*. All her life Mary loved games of chance. She also learnt embroidery, which she enjoyed doing for the rest of her life. People at court were expected to compose their own songs and poems, and so Mary wrote verses with help from a famous poet called Pierre Ronsard. She was taught music and learned to play well on the harp, the *lute* and the *virginals*. Everyone danced at the French court too, and Henry II provided her with a dancing-master who taught her to dance the slow and stately *pavane* and the lively jig and *galliard*.

Learning to do all these things was part of Mary's education. Of course, she had to spend a lot of time in the school-room too. She spoke French most of the time and learnt English,

Ma Dame i'ai esté bien aise d'auoir le moien de vous pouuoir ecrire de
mes nouuelles estant en bien grand peine d'estre si long temps sans en
entendre des votres. Ma dame i'ai entendu que le Gouuerneur s'est mis
en votre volunté, et vous a remis entre mains les placas principales du
roiaume, de quoi ie suis tres aise et en loue tous les iours votre seigneur
et aussi de quoi tous les princes et grands seigneurs sont retornes a vous.
Ie suis arriuée a meudon aupres de ma dame ma grand mere pour faire
la feste de pasques, pource qu'elle, et mon oncle monsieur le cardinal
sont d'aduis que ie recoiue Dieu, auquel ie supplie tres humblement
me donner la grace si bien commancer. Ie ne vueil oblier vous dire
que ce present porteur a fait bon et agreable seruice au Roy.
Ma dame en cest endroit ie vous presenterai mes tres humbles recomman-
dations a votre bonne grace, suppliant le createur vous donner en longue
sante treschureuse vie.

Votre tres humble et tres obeisante fille

MARIE

A letter from Mary written in French to her mother when she was about twelve. It is in the italic style which was fairly new at this time. See if you can read any of the letter

Spanish, Italian, Greek, Latin, as well as studying history and geography. Like every educated person at this time, she had to know enough Latin to be able to read learned books and even to speak it. Once she had to make a speech to the whole court in Latin. The subject was 'that it is suitable for women to study all forms of learning', and everybody said that she spoke it very well.

People at the French court really loved books and learning. This was the time of the *Renaissance*, when people were taking a great interest in the learning and art of ancient Greece and Rome. Mary would have found in the King's library rare books and priceless *manuscripts* written in Latin and Greek hundreds of years before. In his picture gallery she would see beautiful pictures and pieces of sculpture. She learnt to love books and pictures. All this was part of her education.

ROYAL WEDDING

Meanwhile, outside France, things were happening that were to alter Mary's life. In England, King Edward VI died in 1553. His half-sister, Mary Tudor, became Queen and married Philip II of Spain, thus making England and Spain allies in a war against France. So the French needed all the more to hold on to Scotland as an ally. Since 1554 Mary of Guise had been ruling Scotland as regent in place of the unreliable Earl of Arran. But her power was weak. So, to bring Scotland more firmly under French control, arrangements were made in 1558 to hurry on the marriage of Mary Queen of Scots to the Dauphin Francis who would one day be King of France.

Mary and Francis had grown up together almost like brother and sister. They were very fond of each other, although in some ways they were not well matched. Mary's portraits show that by 1558 she was a very attractive young woman of sixteen. She had bright golden hair and an oval face with a pale, creamy skin, a long thin nose and dark, almond-shaped eyes. She was very tall, probably about 1.8 metres. She also carried herself very erect. How different from her future husband! Francis was small for his age, and though he spent most of his time out hunting, he had dull eyes and a puffy face and was never very well.

The wedding took place on 24 April in the great *cathedral* of Notre Dame in Paris. On that day Mary became Dauphine of France as well as Queen of Scots. Since there had not been a wedding ceremony for a dauphin in France for two hundred years, King Henry said that this was to be 'the most famous ever celebrated'.

The people of Paris had never seen such a magnificent sight. It was a public holiday and the narrow streets were crowded with happy townsfolk. Everywhere fluttered banners embroidered with the French royal emblem, the silver *fleur-de-lys* on a blue background. A vast open-air stand for spectators had been set up in front of the cathedral.

Imagine that you arrive in good time to watch the guests arriving in their gorgeous clothes. All of them disappear inside the huge church. If you could follow them inside you would hear choirs singing and see the sunlight streaming through stained glass windows on to priceless church hangings, gold crosses, and the satins, velvets and furs of the congregation. Suddenly, at eleven o'clock there is a fanfare of trumpets. Slowly the stately bridal procession moves towards the cathedral along a bright red carpet. Led by the King's guards, come courtiers, musicians, members of the royal family and the bridegroom with his brothers. The crowds cheer. At last comes the bride herself with the French King, dressed in a scarlet robe lined with gold, leading her by the hand. She is tall and beautiful, and wears a silver gown under a purple *mantle* embroidered with gold. Diamonds sparkle at her neck, while on her head she wears a golden *coronet* glistening with *sapphires*, *rubies* and pearls.

The marriage ceremony takes place at the entrance to the cathedral. Then the King presents his new daughter-in-law to the cheering crowds. The Duke of Guise, who has been in charge of the wedding celebrations, goes about throwing handfuls of gold and silver. With whoops of joy, the pushing, scrambling crowds tumble about on the ground trying to catch the money. A young Scotsman who was actually there tells us what happened:

> Gentlemen lost their cloaks, ladies their *farthingales*, merchants their gowns, teachers their hoods, students their pointed caps, and religious men had their *cassocks* violently torn from their shoulders. It was a merry sport for him that lost nothing. And then to hear their *lamentations* it was no less sport, some saying, 'I have lost my cloak worth ten crowns and got but a *testoon*'. An other says, 'Alas, my gown was plucked from my back, worth six crowns, and I got but five *sous*'. The third says, 'My purse is gone, and fifty crowns in it, and I got nothing'.

Mary, aged seventeen, about the time she married Francis and became Dauphine of France

The rest of that memorable day was spent in feasting and dancing.

Back in Scotland there were also celebrations for the Queen's wedding, though not so grand. In Edinburgh there was a *pageant* and a salute was fired from the big cannon known as Mons Meg. The shot landed two miles away near the sea at Granton.

People in Scotland would not have been nearly so happy if they had known about secret papers that Mary signed about the time of her wedding. These said that if she and her husband died without having any children, Scotland was then to be ruled by the next king of France, 'until he be paid and fully *reimbursed* in a million of gold or such other sums' to make up for 'those *outlays* and expenses *incurred* in the maintenance, defence and protection' of Scotland. Can you see why this agreement was kept secret? If Scottish people had known about it some would have said that their Queen was handing over their country to France. They would never be able to pay up such large sums of money. So Scotland would become just like a part of France. Other people, however, might have said that this was better than being conquered by the English and made part of England.

RETURN TO SCOTLAND

In June 1559 the peace of Mary's happy and sheltered life was suddenly shattered. Francis and she were watching King Henry taking part in a tournament. Suddenly they saw his opponent's lance pierce the King's armour. He was badly wounded in the head and neck, and within days he was dead. The Dauphin unexpectedly became King of France, as Francis II, and Mary became Queen of France. She was now Queen of two countries.

Within a year and a half Mary suffered another blow. Neither she nor her husband had much to do with how France was ruled. The men who really ruled France were Mary's two uncles, the Duke of Guise and his brother. Francis still preferred to spend most of his days out in the hunting field. It was while he was out hunting that he caught a bad chill. Prayers were said for him, doctors did what little they could to help him, and Mary nursed him day and night. But his health had been weak all his short life. Shortly afterwards he died. So, early in December 1560, Mary became a widow when she was only eighteen.

Mary was among the spectators at this tournament in which her father-in-law, Henry II, was badly wounded and later died

What was she to do now? Stay on in France and live quietly on one of her many estates? Get married again to a foreign ruler? Many men wanted to marry her but she was not interested in any of them. Even her young brother-in-law, the new King of France, Charles IX, thought about making her his wife. But Mary did not get on with his mother, Queen Catherine, so there was nothing for it but to return to Scotland. There Mary of Guise had died the year before, leaving the country without any strong ruler. There had been a civil war. Mary knew that she would have many problems to face in Scotland but she would at least be Queen in her own country and not an ex-queen as in France. She therefore made up her mind to return to Scotland.

At eight o'clock on the morning of 14 August 1561, with a heavy mist hanging over the sea, Mary set sail from the port of Calais for home. Her days in France were over and a new life awaited her in Scotland.

3   *A Bad Time for the Catholic Church*

While Mary had been living in France two great changes had taken place in Scotland: the official religion of the country had been changed from Roman Catholic to Protestant, and England had become Scotland's ally instead of France. Politics and religion were very closely bound up with each other in the sixteenth century.

WHAT WAS WRONG WITH THE CATHOLIC CHURCH?

To understand how these changes came about we shall have to go back to the time when Mary's father, James V of Scotland, was still King. Then everybody throughout western Europe belonged to the one Church, the Catholic Church, with the Pope at its head living in Rome. During the time of James V, however, many people in Europe stopped believing in the Catholic Church. They felt that churchmen had grown too fond of money and power in this world and that the leaders of the Church set a very bad example.

In Scotland, it was the King and not the Pope who appointed *bishops* and *abbots*. But instead of choosing men who led simple lives the King chose men who would help him to rule the country. This was because he did not have enough money to pay his advisers. James V had an income of about £45,000: the Church in Scotland had about £300,000 a year, which came from taxes paid to the Church and from land that it owned. Cardinal Beaton, whom you read about in Chapter 1, was one of these churchmen. He was Archbishop of St Andrews and head of all the *clergy* in Scotland; but he spent much of his time working for James V as his *chancellor*, or chief adviser.

This meant, of course, that he could not attend to his duties in the Church and so these were often not done.

King James got money from the Church in another way. When an abbot died the King sometimes put off making a new one in his place. This gave him the chance to use the money which came from the *monastery* lands. He might keep the money for himself, but often he would reward one of his nobles by making him responsible for looking after the monastery. This man was known as a *commendator*. As commendator he was supposed to take care of the monastery estates for the benefit of the Church until the King chose a new abbot. Usually, however, he treated the estates as if they were his very own. So the commendators were mainly interested in getting as much money as possible out of the monasteries. They did not pay much attention to what went on inside them. In the abbeys of Culross and Kinloss, both ruled by abbots, praying and learning went as before, but in most of the others, run

Dryburgh Abbey, as it might have looked in the sixteenth century. This was one of the Border Abbeys that were badly damaged during the 'Rough Wooing'

by commendators, the monks were very lazy and led lives
that were anything but holy. In his famous pageant play,
'A *Satire* of *the Three Estates*', Sir David Lindsay pokes fun at
the monks by making an abbot say:

> My monks and I, we live right easily:
> There are no monks, from Carrick to Crail,
> That fare better, and drink more wholesome ale.
> My *prior* is a man of great devotion;
> Therefore, daily, he gets a double *portion*...
> My *paramours* are both as fat and fair
> As any *wench* in the town of Ayr.
> I send my sons to Paris, to the schools,
> I trust in God that they shall be no fools.
> And all my daughters I have well provided;
> Now, judge you, if my office be well guided.

Nuns were just as bad. After inspecting Scottish convents the
Pope's special *representative*, Cardinal Sermonetta, reported:

> Not only do the nuns wander outside the *monastic* enclosures
> in shameless fashion through the houses of *seculars*, but even
> admit all sorts of worthless and wicked men within their
> convents. They *defile* the sacred *precincts* with the birth
> of children and bring up their *progeny* about them, go
> forth surrounded by their numerous sons, and give their
> daughters in marriage *dowered with* the simple *revenues* of the
> Church.

Money, money, money! You might think that churchmen were
always talking about money. This was because they had to
pay so much to the Pope and to the King in taxes. In fact,
the Church helped to pay for the running of the country. About
half the taxes that King James received came from the Church.

Since so much of the Church's wealth was being taken away
the monasteries were no longer able to carry on with their
work of caring for the old, the sick and the poor. Also, there
was little money to pay for the repair of monastery buildings.
Many parish churches were in just as bad a state. In Berwick-

shire, for instance, it was reported that some did not have any walls or windows and that the roofs were ready to collapse. At Coldingham the roof had actually fallen in, and on wet days the priest had to take services under a canopy draped over the altar.

Many parish churches had been handed over to monasteries. The monks chose a *vicar* to do the work of the parish priest. Often they paid him so little that not many priests were willing to take on the job. So the vicar was sometimes very badly educated, neither able to preach well nor even knowing enough Latin to say the church services. If you remember that 85 per cent of parish churches had been handed over to monasteries as well as to cathedrals, universities and churches in towns, you will understand why religion was in such a bad way.

When so many priests were ignorant, education suffered too. In many parishes the priest was also the local 'dominie', or schoolmaster. Many priests were so poor that they even took on more than one parish to earn more money. This was known as *pluralism*.

Priests also demanded special offerings at Christmas and Easter, and insisted on being paid extra for performing services at weddings, baptisms and funerals. People thought the priests were just being greedy. One payment that people hated most of all was the 'corpse present' when their relatives died. We can see this in Sir David Lindsay's play, 'A Satire of the Three Estates' mentioned earlier. On to the stage comes a poor man dressed in filthy rags. He tells how he and his family were once quite well off until disaster struck:

> My father was so weak of blood and bane (bone),
> That he deit (died), wherefore my mother made great
> > mane (moan).
>
> Then she deit within a day or two,
> And then began my poverty and woe.
> Our good grey mare (horse) was baitand (grazing) on the field

And our land's laird took her for his hereild (lord's due),
Our vicar took the best cow by the heid (head)
Incontinent (immediately), when my father was deid
(dead).
And when the vicar heard tell how that my mother
Was deid, fra-hand (straight away) he took fra (from)
me another.
Then Meg my wife did murn (mourn) baith even and
morrow
Till at the last she deit for very sorrow.
And when the vicar heard tell my wife was deid,
The thrid (third) cow he cleikit (seized) by the heid.
Their umest clais (uppermost clothes) that were of
rapploch (homespun) grey,
The vicar gart (made) his clerk beir (bear) them away.
When all was gane (gone) I micht mak na debate (might
not argue),
But with my bairns (children) passed for to beg my meat.

Many people had some reason for disliking the Church. Kings were jealous of the Pope's power and influence. Nobles did not like the fact that people still paid respect to bishops and abbots. Merchants, craftsmen and other ordinary people were annoyed that they had to work hard for their living while monks and priests seemed to do no work at all. All of them thought that the Church had too much wealth and they could not wait to grab hold of it for themselves.

HOW THE REFORMATION CAME TO SCOTLAND
In the past many people had tried to make the lives of church-men better, that is, to *reform* the Church. But it was not easy to put things right, because if people found fault with the Church the clergy might accuse them of *heresy*. Nearly every-body at this time believed that there was only one way to think about God and that was through obeying the Church's teach-ing; if you disagreed you could be put to death as a *heretic*. Yet sometimes faults had been put right, and afterwards the Church had been all the better for the changes made. But now

in the sixteenth century in other countries in Europe, as well as in Scotland, the Church's weaknesses were so great that when people tried to reform the Church, it broke in pieces. In place of the one Catholic Church there grew up many reformed, or Protestant Churches, each under its own head, alongside the Roman Catholic Church still under the Pope.

This *Reformation* started in Germany in 1517, when a monk named Martin Luther quarrelled with the Pope and was supported by many of the German princes. (You can read all about him in another 'Then and There' book, 'Luther and the Reformation'.) Soon the Germans were divided into those who stayed loyal to the Pope and the Roman Catholic Church, and those, whom we call Protestants, who agreed with Luther and his supporters.

It was not long before the Reformation came to Scotland. The new ideas were brought by trading ships. Many ships sailed between German ports and Scotland, usually bringing metal goods, timber and cloth. But now they carried also bundles of books. Thanks to the invention of the printing-press which meant books could be made quickly and cheaply, Luther's ideas were spreading fast all over Europe.

Ships' captains soon found that books were a dangerous cargo. In 1525 a law was passed against 'the *damnable* opinions spread by the heretic Luther and his *disciples*': anybody found bringing Protestant books into Scotland could be put in prison and have his ship and its cargo taken away from him. But people still wanted to read these books, especially copies of the New Testament in English. Until recently the Bible had been written in Latin, which meant that only priests and the few educated people who knew Latin could read it. Now more and more people were demanding to read the Bible in their own language. The Church did not want people to read it for themselves in case they did not understand it properly. But in spite of what churchmen said, scholars began to translate the Bible into modern languages. So, from ships off the coast sailors smuggled English New Testaments ashore and passed them on to people to read at home.

4 'The Reek of Master Hamilton'

By 1528 so many people in Scotland were reading Protestant books that the rulers of the country became very alarmed. They decided to make an example of a young Protestant preacher called Patrick Hamilton, even though he belonged to a very powerful family. Since the age of fifteen he had been Abbot of Fearn in Angus. Most young noblemen placed in charge of an abbey to give them an income were not interested in religion. But Patrick Hamilton was different. He studied *theology* first at St Andrews and then at foreign universities. Then he wrote a religious book which churchmen said was heretical. To avoid arrest he fled abroad. When he thought it was safe he returned and became laird of an estate near Linlithgow. Soon he was preaching Protestant ideas among his tenants. The Archbishop of St Andrews heard of this, and so Patrick Hamilton was led off to the Archbishop's palace to be questioned about his religious beliefs.

There he was put on trial for heresy, found guilty and sentenced to death. Normally such a trial lasted for many weeks. During this time the accused person was patiently questioned by learned men who tried to show him why they thought he was wrong; finally, if he refused to give up his beliefs he was swiftly put to death. The trial of Patrick Hamilton was over in twelve hours, but his execution was long and painful.

On the afternoon of 29 February 1528 in St Andrews a crowd of people gathered to watch Hamilton as he was led out and tied to a stake in front of St Salvator's College. Timber, coal and bundles of straw were neatly laid out around him. The fire was lit, smoke and flames gathered about him. All

the time people were desperately trying to make him change
his ideas and beg for mercy. Grimly he refused. Then a terrible
thing happened. The gunpowder placed underneath the
kindling suddenly exploded. It was meant to make the fire
burn all the more quickly, but instead it scorched the left side
of his face and blew off his left hand. So, for the next six hours
as the fire smouldered on, Patrick Hamilton remained conscious
as he slowly burned to death.

*A heretic
being burnt at
the stake*

Putting Patrick Hamilton to death did not do the Church
any good. One of the Archbishop's friends said: 'My lord, if
you burn any more heretics you will utterly destroy yourselves;
for the *reek* of Master Hamilton has infected as many as it
blew upon.' What he meant was that instead of stopping the
spread of Protestant ideas, the burning of Patrick Hamilton
only made people want to know all the more about them.

Imagine yourself standing in the High Street of a small
Scottish town about this time. You join a crowd gathered
about the *mercat cross*. A preacher like Patrick Hamilton is

speaking. You hear him say that God and not the Pope is the head of all Christians because the Bible did not say anything about a pope. People do not need to pray to saints, he says, to go on *pilgrimages* or do good works such as giving money to the Church so as to make sure their souls go to heaven. As the Bible says, all you need is faith in God's mercy. The preacher talks of all the things that Reformers say are wrong with church services. When the priest is saying *mass* the bread and wine do not actually turn into the body and blood of Christ, as the Church teaches, Protestant reformers say that these are only *symbols* to help people understand why Jesus died. Besides, they say, it should not be only the priest who eats the bread and drinks the wine; all the people should join in the service as a sign that Christ saved them. There are many other things that reformers say are wrong: praying in front of statues of saints is *idolatrous* and paying special respect to the Virgin Mary is *blasphemous*. Altogether, reformers want a church in which people worship in the way the first Christians were told to worship in the New Testament.

All over southern Scotland people began to talk about these Protestant ideas. Some heard about them by listening to preachers, others by reading books and *pamphlets* that were soon grubby and torn with being passed from hand to hand so much. They also got to know about new ideas from watching stage-plays, acted in the open air. You have already read some lines from the most famous of these plays, 'A Satire of the Three Estates'.

GEORGE WISHART

As long as James V was alive he remained loyal to the Pope and sent reformers to be burned at the stake. Many reformers must have sighed with relief, therefore, when James died in 1542 and the Earl of Arran became Governor of Scotland for the little Mary Queen of Scots. Arran let the Reformers alone and allowed people to read the Bible in English. In fact, the English ambassador reported that English Bibles were so much in demand that 'if there were a cart-load sent *thither* they would be bought every one'. It was a pity, however, that many Reformers used their newfound freedom badly. They went about in mobs, breaking into monasteries and smashing up *images* of saints. But all this was stopped, when Cardinal Beaton made himself the real ruler of Scotland and brought back again the harsh laws against the Reformers.

A young preacher from Montrose called George Wishart, after spending five years in exile, returned to Scotland in 1543. Now he went about openly preaching Protestant ideas in Angus, Fife and Ayrshire. Eager crowds followed him everywhere. Sometimes he held services in churches, other times in the open air. He never spent long in one place because he knew that at any moment he might be taken prisoner. He was always surrounded by an armed bodyguard.

The Protestant preacher, George Wishart, in 1543 aged thirty, three years before he was burnt at the stake in St Andrews

If you had attended one of Wishart's services you would have seen a tall, neatly dressed young man, with short dark hair and a black beard, speaking to the crowd. A mild-tempered kind of man you might have thought him, until he began to preach. Then you would have seen his face darken and his eyes flash as he spoke out against the evils of the Church.

It was fiery preaching like this that drew such large crowds. In ordinary church services, remember, priests did not often preach at all. There was not much singing either. But here, at Protestant services, people could let themselves go in singing psalms and hymns, many of which were set to popular tunes of the time. These hymns and psalms of the early Scottish Reformers are known as 'The *Guid* and Godly Ballads'.

At last when George Wishart was bold enough to preach very near the court at Edinburgh, Cardinal Beaton ordered his arrest. In January 1546 Wishart was preaching in and around Haddington while staying at Ormiston. Suddenly one night soldiers surrounded the house and took Wishart away without a struggle. After a short trial in which he calmly defended himself and said he had done no wrong, he was found guilty of heresy. On 1 March 1546 he was first strangled and then burnt to ashes in front of the Cardinal's castle at St Andrews. Within a few months his followers took their revenge on the Cardinal by taking part in his murder, which you read about in Chapter 1. Like the execution of Patrick Hamilton eighteen years earlier, the burning of George Wishart only added to the growing number of Protestants.

JOHN KNOX

One of the people who joined the murderers of Cardinal Beaton when they shut themselves up in St Andrews Castle was John Knox who did more than anyone to make the Reformation in Scotland. On the next page you see what is probably the only true portrait of Knox, although the artist painted it from memory some years after Knox was dead. Knox was a short, broad-shouldered man, with a dark ruddy complexion, black hair and a thick black beard. Someone who knew him said that he had a look about him that was 'grave and stern, but not harsh'.

We know quite a lot about what Knox did because he wrote a book, called 'The History of the Reformation in Scotland', which is mostly about Knox's part in the Reformation. He does not tell us much about his early life, however. It is likely that he was born in Haddington in 1514. When he was about seven he was probably sent to the local *song-school* run by monks, who would have taught him some reading, a little religious knowledge and how to sing in their church choir. The monks would probably see that he was a bright lad and that it was worthwhile training him to be a priest. At this time there was little else that an intelligent boy from a poor home could do. But like many other young priests around this time, Knox found himself without a job. There were too many priests and not enough churches. Fortunately he was able to find work as a kind of lawyer known as a *notary*. To make more money he sometimes worked as a private tutor to the families of local lairds.

While he was teaching in East Lothian he met George Wishart who encouraged him to work for the reform of the Church. He became Wishart's bodyguard and carried a long, two-handed sword. When Wishart was arrested Knox wanted to stay and defend him, but Wishart sent him away, saying,

'Nay, return to your *bairns*, and God bless you. One is sufficient for a sacrifice.'

To avoid arrest Knox joined those Reformers who had shut themselves in St Andrews Castle. While he was teaching the children religious knowledge one of the leaders of the Reformers noticed how passionately he spoke and asked him to preach to them. Though he had been trained as a priest, Knox had never taken a service before. So he preached to a congregation for the first time in the parish church of St Andrews. Everybody present agreed that here was a man worth listening to.

In the summer of 1547 when the French finally forced the defenders to surrender the castle of St Andrews they took Knox away with them to serve in their *galleys*. He does not say much about this time in his book, probably because he wanted to forget about it. No sailors ever chose to serve in these ships, as life was so hard, so they had to be manned by either convicts or prisoners of war. Knox was a galley-slave for nineteen months. He spent most of his time on board ship in the river Loire, but once he took part in an expedition to his native land, and was able to see the spire of the church in St Andrews. On this voyage he became dangerously ill. As a result he suffered bad health for the rest of his days.

But life on the galleys cannot have been as bad for Knox as for others. He was able to keep in touch with other Scottish prisoners and had enough time off to write a copy of a religious book. Except for the times when he would not attend mass and refused to pay respect to a statue of the Virgin Mary, he was able to stay out of trouble. He was determined to survive in order to carry out his great ambition, the reformation of the Church in Scotland.

At long last in the spring of 1549 Knox was released from the French galleys. But he was not allowed to return home, and so he spent the next ten years outside Scotland. First he went to live in England. It was the time when Protestant noblemen governed the country in the name of young Edward VI. Knox was treated as an honoured guest. He became minister of the church in Berwick-upon-Tweed, and from there he was able to hear about events in Scotland. But news of his sincere preaching soon reached London and he was invited to become one of the royal *chaplains*. Then Edward VI died, and his Catholic sister, Mary, became Queen in 1553. Mary wanted to make England Roman Catholic again. Like other rulers in the sixteenth century she put Protestants to death. Knox was therefore a marked man. He had to move about from one place to another to avoid capture. Finally in January 1554 he left England and fled for safety across the Channel.

He spent most of the next five years abroad as minister of a church for English refugees, which settled at Geneva in Switzerland. Here he met the great Protestant thinker, John Calvin, who gave him many new ideas. Calvin was a Frenchman who, like Knox, had fled to Geneva looking for religious freedom. Now he was a powerful leader of the Protestant Church there.

Calvin's church was not like other Protestant churches. Those Churches which followed the teaching of Martin Luther, in Denmark, Sweden and the German states, were ruled by kings or princes through the bishops whom they appointed. But in Geneva the ministers ruled the church themselves, helped by men chosen from the congregation known as elders. Since the Greek word for elder is 'presbyteros' this kind of Church is called *presbyterian*. It was this kind of church which Knox set up in Scotland.

One thing that Knox admired about Calvin's Church was its strict discipline. Calvin believed that people had to be ruled strictly to make them lead godly lives. So, if you had visited Geneva at this time you might have seen this notice on the wall of your inn:

> The inn-keeper shall not allow any *loose-living* like dancing, dice or cards, nor receive anyone suspected of any such loose-living.

46   If you fancied going out for the evening you would have to be

in early because no one was allowed to stay up after nine o'clock at night. To get people to obey such stern laws Calvin used spies to report those who misbehaved and they were severely punished. Other churches tried to make people live according to their rules but none was so successful as Calvin's church at Geneva. Knox described it as 'the most perfect school of Christ that ever was in earth since the days of the *Apostles*'.

THE CHURCH TRIES TO REFORM ITSELF

During these years that Knox spent abroad he looked forward eagerly to letters from friends who gave news from Scotland. This was the time, you remember, when Mary Queen of Scots was being brought up in France and when her mother, Mary of Guise, was ruling Scotland with French help. Mary of Guise was a loyal Catholic but she was also interested in trying to reform the Church. So were some of the Church leaders. If you had been one of Knox's friends you might have told him about an important meeting of Church leaders in the church of the Greyfriars in Edinburgh in 1549. This was a meeting of the *Provincial Council* of Scotland, which included learned men from the universities as well as bishops and abbots. The Council sat for many months discussing what was wrong with the Church. At last it agreed that its troubles were due to two main causes: many churchmen were badly educated and they led wicked lives.

What was to be done? The Provincial Council made some rules for the future. Schools were to be set up in cathedrals to teach priests Latin, *divinity* and *canon law* so that they would be able to answer the learned arguments of Reformers. Clergymen were to be more carefully chosen; they were not to hold more than one *living* at a time and they were to preach more often. They were also to lead purer lives. This meant eating less, dressing more simply and getting rid of their *concubines*.

Two years later the Provincial Council met again. Sadly it had to admit that its rules were not being carried out, and so it issued them again. But it did something else. Realising that

47

people did not know enough about the Church's teaching, the Provincial Council now ordered that a *catechism* should be issued. This was to be a 'plain and easy statement and explanation of the *rudiments* of the faith', written in simple Scots so that everybody could understand it.

The Catechism was written by Archbishop John Hamilton of St Andrews. Copies were sent to all parishes. Priests were told to read out parts of it in church every Sunday and on holy days 'for the space of half an hour before high mass in a loud and *audible* voice distinctly, without stammering, lest they expose themselves to the ridicule of their hearers', (that is, make themselves look stupid). Hamilton tried in his catechism to please Protestants as well as Catholics. If Protestants read it they would find much in it that was like their own beliefs. But the catechism came too late to save the Church. Many nobles, lairds and townsfolk, especially in eastern Scotland, were already openly attending Protestant church services.

MARY OF GUISE AND THE LORDS OF THE CONGREGATION
In their letters to John Knox friends would tell him also about changes in the government of Scotland. In 1554 the Earl of Arran was finally persuaded to resign as Governor, and Mary of Guise was now formally made regent in his place. You can see what this meant. The French were now trying to get Scotland within their power. But if Scotland was to be of any use to France Mary of Guise saw that she would have to keep the country peaceful and not divided over arguments about religion. So she did her best to keep on the right side of the nobles, especially those who sided with the Protestants. She did this by giving them French gold and allowing those who were commendators to hold on to their Church lands. She even let Protestants worship freely. All this was useful to France because, for the moment at least, it kept the nobles loyal. But in the long run it did the Church no good. Can you see why?

Hearing about these changes made Knox decide in the autumn of 1555 that it was safe to return to Scotland. So for

the next ten months he went about preaching in those parts
of the country – Angus, Fife, Lothian and Ayrshire – where
the Protestants were strongest. This frightened the Church
leaders. They saw that if Knox went on preaching like this
people would no longer obey them, so they decided that he
would have to be stopped. They summoned him to stand
trial for heresy in Edinburgh. Mary of Guise, however, was
afraid that he might come at the head of an army of followers,
and so she persuaded the Church leaders to call off the trial.
Knox still came to Edinburgh, however, and preached in the

*Mary of Guise,
mother of Mary
Queen of Scots, who
was Queen Regent
of Scotland from
1554 until her
death in 1560*

High Street to enthusiastic crowds. The Protestants seemed
to have found a leader at last. They chose him to write a letter
to the Queen Regent, asking her to become a Protestant, or
at least allow Protestants to worship in complete freedom.
Mary of Guise now saw that being gentle with the Protestants
had not won over the nobles and that she would have to rely
more on the Church's support. So she proudly rejected Knox's
letter.

   Knox realised that he had come back too soon, and returned
to Geneva. Before he left he told his followers how they should   49

carry on without him. They were to hold services in their houses every day, pray together and read passages from the Bible. Lairds and masters were to explain difficult words to their tenants and servants. In this way Knox hoped to build up the strong support among the common people that he needed to bring about a successful Protestant Reformation.

More and more of the nobles and lairds were becoming Protestant now, although for different reasons. Many became Protestant because they thought that Mary of Guise was treating Scotland as if it belonged to France. French soldiers manned the important castles and French nobles held high positions in the government. By 1557 the French were so unpopular in Scotland that when Mary of Guise tried to raise an army to invade England the nobles refused to go. In the next year, as you read in Chapter 2, the marriage of the young Queen Mary with the Dauphin was suddenly hurried on to bring Scotland even more tightly under French control. Their hatred of France was making many Scottish nobles side with the Protestants against Mary of Guise and her ally, the Catholic Church.

In December 1557 the leading Protestant nobles formed themselves into a group which they called 'the Congregation of Christ'. These *Lords of the Congregation*, as they were called, promised to fight if necessary to make Scotland a Protestant country. In 1558 the Church leaders did a very foolish thing which helped the Protestants. Nobody in Scotland had been put to death for his religion since 1550. But now an eighty-eight-year-old priest, Walter Myln, was burnt at the stake in St Andrews, for teaching scripture, churchmen said, to the children of a widow in Dysart. When the crowds saw the frail old man standing writhing in the flames they burst through the ring of soldiers to cut through his ropes and put him out of his agony. By the time the Provincial Council met again in the spring of 1559 to make more changes, everybody knew that it was too late to make peaceful reforms in the Church. A *revolution* was about to break loose that would sweep the old Church in Scotland away.

5 *Protestant Victory*

In 1559 Protestants and Catholics in Scotland alike looked for help from abroad. The Queen Regent counted on more help from France now that young Queen Mary had married the Dauphin in the previous April. In England the death of Mary Tudor in November 1558 meant that the Protestant Elizabeth was now Queen. This encouraged the Lords of the Congregation to hope for English help. On 1 January 1559 a notice, known as 'the Beggars' *Summons*' mysteriously appeared on the doors of the *friaries* throughout Scotland. It ordered the 'flocks of friars' to clear out of their houses and leave them to those who really needed them: 'the blind, the *crooked*, the bed-ridden, widows, orphans and other people who were out of work'. Soon, people in Dundee, Perth, St Andrews and other towns were openly saying that they were in favour of the new reformed *Kirk*.

Mary of Guise at last decided to take firm action against Protestants. At Easter she ordered everybody to attend the old church services. She also ordered some Protestant preachers to come to Stirling to answer charges of heresy and outlawed them when they did not come. Angry crowds gathered in Perth. There they were joined by John Knox who had just returned from abroad. On 11 May in the church of St John they listened to him preaching a burning sermon against the worship of idols. At the end of the service the church was almost empty when a priest came in to say mass. A boy made a rude remark and the priest struck him. The boy threw a stone. It missed the priest and hit an image. People drifted back to see what was happening. They began throwing stones too.

Soon all the images in the church were broken. Then 'the rascal *multitude*', as Knox called them, rushed out and burned down the houses of friars, after first making off with their food and bed-clothes. All over southern Scotland it was the same: churches were stripped of their statues, richly carved woodwork and stained glass windows, while beautiful embroidered altar clothes and *vestments* were either stolen or destroyed. Many of the people who helped to destroy the churches honestly believed that they were cleansing them of evil.

Meanwhile, Protestants and Catholics had both gathered armies, although neither side seemed to want to fight. Each was playing for time until foreign help arrived. The Queen Regent hoped the French would send help, and the Lords of the Congregation waited for the English to send help. In 1559 young Queen Mary had become Queen of France. Now her mother was certain that she would get more men and supplies from France. Sure enough, within a few weeks 1,000 French troops landed at Leith to reinforce the 3,000 already in Scotland. With the soldiers came their wives and children, showing that they intended to stay for a long time. The Lords of the Congregation looked on in dismay. Their army was small and badly disciplined. What hope had they now of driving out the French and setting up a reformed Kirk? Desperately they begged Queen Elizabeth of England to send help quickly.

Elizabeth took a long time to make up her mind. She thought it wrong to help foreign rebels, which is what the Lords of the Congregation were. She would not have liked it if a foreign ruler had helped rebels against her. So if you had been one of her advisers you might have said that Elizabeth should not take a part in Scottish affairs.

On the other hand, she could not ignore Scotland. If the Lords of the Congregation did not get help soon the Catholic French would win and be able to use Scotland as a base for attacking Protestant England whenever they liked. Then they would be able to force Elizabeth off the throne and make Mary Queen of Scots ruler of England in her place. If you

*The siege of Leith, 1560. You are looking southwards from the Firth of Forth
towards Arthur's Seat and the Pentland Hills in the background. Pick out
Edinburgh with its castle, the English camp on the left, and the English trenches
surrounding Leith in the centre foreground*

look at the family tree on page 8 you will see that Mary was
a cousin of Elizabeth. Already the French had said that Mary
was the rightful Queen of England because she was a Catholic.
So, to protect England, Elizabeth finally made up her mind
to help the Scottish Protestants. In February 1560 Scottish
and English leaders signed a treaty at Berwick: it said that
Elizabeth would send an army to drive the French out of
Scotland. After centuries of fighting against each other
Scottish and English soldiers were now to fight on the same side.

An English army, 9,000 strong, entered Scotland and began
to besiege the French in the port of Leith, while English
ships kept up a *blockade* off-shore. Leith was strongly defended,
and from its church steeples the French gunners could train　53

their deadly fire on to the English as they tried to creep along in their trenches and lay mines under the walls. Almost every day they were able to come out and drive the English back. But the English had better guns. Out on the *links* to the east they built large mounds of earth from which to fire them. The remains of these mounds, Mount Pelham and Mount Somerset, named after English artillery captains, can still be seen to this day. From these and other positions as well as from their ships, the English poured blazing shot into the port. Many of the defenders suffered from disease and died of starvation after eating their horses and surviving on shellfish.

The French saw that it was pointless to carry on fighting: it was Mary of Guise who insisted on still holding out. But by now she was dying in Edinburgh Castle, her body horribly swollen with *dropsy*. In June 1560, she died and English and French leaders met to discuss a cease-fire. Early in July they signed an agreement known as the Treaty of Edinburgh. It said that each side was to withdraw its troops from Scotland. It was also agreed that no foreigner (meaning of course, no Frenchman) should be a member of the Scottish government. It also said that Mary Queen of Scots was to give up calling herself Queen of England. So, the Treaty of Edinburgh ended the Auld Alliance between Scotland and France and also ended the fighting between Scotland and the 'Auld Enemy', England. This treaty is an important turning-point in history. From now on Scotland and England started to be more friendly, sharing the same religion.

THE NEW KIRK

Nothing was said about religion in the Treaty of Edinburgh. Both sides wisely agreed that the Scots should decide this for themselves. The Scottish Parliament was therefore summoned. Early in August 1560 noblemen, lairds and men from the burghs made their way to Edinburgh. Many of the lairds had never sat in Parliament before. But they came now to show that they wanted a say in the affairs of the country because

 many of them were Protestants.

This meeting is sometimes called 'the Reformation Parliament'. It was one of the most important in Scotland's history. It passed laws which made Scotland Protestant. The rule of the Pope was done away with and the saying of mass was declared to be against the law. The new laws said that people who attended mass were to have all their property taken away. If they continued to attend mass in secret, they could be put to death.

Parliament also approved the Confession of Faith. This was a statement which set down in writing the religious beliefs of the new Protestant Church which were taken from the Bible. Protestant ministers were appointed to churches in various parts of the country: John Knox became minister of St Giles's in Edinburgh, which people looked on as the most important church in all Scotland.

It was John Knox who drew up the Confession of Faith. He also wrote 'The Book of Discipline'. This was a plan of how the new Kirk ought to be organised and run. He got his ideas from John Calvin. The Book of Discipline said that ministers were to be chosen by members of their congregation and that laymen called elders and *deacons* should be chosen, the elders to 'assist the minister in all public affairs of the Church', such as carrying out the Church's laws, while the deacons were to see that its money was properly spent. When the minister, elders and deacons of a parish met they made up what was called the kirk session. This was the presbyterian form of Church government which Knox had admired in Calvin's Geneva. Do you remember why it was called presbyterian? You can find out if you turn back to page 46.

Knox knew that many ministers would need help in their work, so he suggested that about ten of the more experienced ministers should be appointed to look after them. He called these men superintendents. Each one would look after the ministers in a particular part of the country, just like a bishop did in his *diocese* in the old Catholic Church. But, said the Book of Discipline, 'these men must not be suffered (allowed) to live as your idle bishops have done *heretofore*'. Superintendents were to preach at least three times a week and travel about their districts to make sure that ministers were doing their work properly.

As you can see, the Reformers were trying to learn from the mistakes and faults of the old Catholic Church. Ministers in the reformed Kirk could marry. The Book of Discipline also said that they should be properly paid, and those with children should have a family allowance. Education was made more important. Ministers were to be well educated and all children were to go to school 'for the virtuous education and godly upbringing of the youth of this realm'. There was to be a school in every parish with a schoolmaster to teach grammar and Latin. The minister himself should teach the children in country districts. He would teach them the catechism, how to read, write and count. When parents were too poor to pay the fees for university, bright children were to be given *bursaries*. You might wonder why Knox and the other Reformers paid so much attention to education. It was so that everybody should be able to read the Bible and play a full part in the running of the Kirk.

Providing education for all, paying decent *stipends* to the ministers as well as caring for the sick, the poor and the aged, would all cost a lot of money. Where was it to come from? The Book of Discipline had the answer: from the old Catholic Church, which, you remember, had lands worth a lot of money. There was one snag, which you have probably spotted. Much of the Church's wealth was in the hands of the lairds and nobles. Even though many of them had supported the Reformation they were not likely to give up these lands willingly. Neither would the government nor the Catholic bishops and priests who still held some of the wealth of the Church. So, although the Book of Discipline was full of excellent ideas the question was, how could they be carried out? The question of who was to get the Church's wealth was only one of the many difficult problems which Mary Queen of Scots would have to tackle when she came back to her own country.

6 Mary's Reign in Scotland: the Successful Years

A heavy *haar* was hanging over the Firth of Forth when Mary Queen of Scots came back to Scotland from France in August 1561. In the words of John Knox: 'The very face of heaven did *manifestly* speak what comfort was brought into this country with her, *to wit*, sorrow, *dolour*, darkness, and all *impiety*.' Fortunately for Mary, not all her subjects looked on her arrival as gloomily as this. Favourable winds had brought her home more quickly than expected, but the sound of her ships' guns soon brought the crowds down to the shore at Leith to welcome her. On 19 August she stepped ashore after thirteen years spent abroad.

Mary's people showed how pleased they were to see her home again. John Knox tells us that on her first night at the Palace of Holyroodhouse, 'Fires of joy were set forth all night, and a company of the most honest, with instruments of music, gave their *salutations* at her chamber window. The melody (as she *alleged*) liked her well; and she willed the same to be continued some nights after.'

A few days later there was a public holiday when she made her official entry into Edinburgh. Crowds lined the High Street, which was decorated with painted arches, while the houses were hung with flowers and bunting. At the mercat cross the wells ran with wine. There were pageants, speeches of welcome and children singing. All the while there was the sound of cheering crowds, the boom of gunfire from the Castle, and 'the noise of people *casting* the glasses of wine' at the mercat cross. Mary spent three weeks at Holyroodhouse. Then she went on a short tour of her kingdom, visiting Linlithgow,

Stirling, Perth, Dundee and St Andrews. Everywhere crowds came out to welcome their twenty-year-old Queen, and said, 'God bless that sweet face'.

But Mary must have thought that Scotland was a very bleak country compared with France. And how small and gloomy she must have found her palaces compared with those she had known in France. But soon she had made them comfortable with the attractive tapestries and soft cushions that she had

The Palace of Holyroodhouse, Edinburgh, as it looked in the sixteenth century. Queen Mary lived in the part with the round turrets on the left

brought home with her. Many of the furnishings were green, her favourite colour. Mary also brought from France many beds. She must have been thankful for their thick hangings to keep out the cold draughts!

Mary tried to carry on the kind of life she had been accustomed to in France. She went hawking and hunting in the woods around Falkland, practised her archery at Stirling and had rounds of golf down at Seton near Prestonpans. Often she was to be seen playing at 'pall mall', as *croquet* was called at this time. Sometimes she strolled about the gardens at Holyrood which she had set out like ones she had known in France.

When it was too wet or cold to go out she still loved to play chess and gamble at cards, dice and backgammon. Music gave her great pleasure. Many an evening she and her courtiers would entertain each other singing and playing on their lutes. Then there were the court festivities at Christmas and Easter. Mary loved to dance. A birthday, a wedding or any celebration was always an excuse for dancing. There were also plenty of opportunities for wearing fancy dress. Mary liked to put on men's costume, and even walked about the streets of Edinburgh dressed like a man; since she was so tall and slim she went about without being recognised. Everywhere she went she was accompanied by those childhood friends, her 'Four Maries'. She would spend many an hour listening to their gossip while busily stitching at her needlework, her favourite pastime.

The English ambassador reported that Mary often did her needlework at meetings of her Privy Council. This was a group of men who advised her how to govern the country. Mary was very careful whom she chose as advisers. Most of them were nobles who were in favour of the Reformation and the Protestant Church. She herself, you will remember, was a Catholic, but she showed that she meant to keep on the right side of those men who had seized control of Scotland from her mother two years before.

Very sensibly also, Mary allowed herself to be guided by two able men who were her chief advisers, Lord James Stewart and Sir William Maitland of Lethington. Lord James was her half-brother, an *illegitimate* son of James V. He was a very stern man and a firm Protestant. He had been one of the leaders of the Lords of the Congregation who fought against Mary of Guise and he was determined that Scotland should remain a Protestant country. Maitland of Lethington was also a Protestant, but he was less interested in religion, and thought that it should not get in the way of how a country was ruled. He served Mary as her Secretary of State. He wanted to make Scotland and England more friendly towards each

other so that the two countries could one day be united under
Mary as queen. These two men were the real rulers of Scotland.

There was much for them to do. Since the death of Mary
of Guise the day-to-day business of government had been
allowed to slide. Take the problem of keeping law and order,
for instance. On the Border many people seemed to have given
up obeying the law altogether. Families such as the Armstrongs,
the Kers, the Scotts and the Elliots went in for raiding farms
and villages across the Border in England as part of their daily
life. English Borderers did the same in Scotland. This raiding
led to constant fighting which in turn caused ill-feeling
between the Scottish and English governments, who seemed
powerless to stop it.

Lord James and Lethington were determined to bring law
and order to the Borders. Lord James rode south at the head
of his men, rounded up many of the Borderers and hanged

*Queen Mary's
half-brother, Lord
James Stewart,
Earl of Moray*

them at the cross in Jedburgh. Thanks to Lord James, Mary was the first ruler to bring some peace to the Border country.

More complicated than keeping law and order, however, was the question of religion. The Reformation Parliament had declared that Scotland was officially Protestant, but Mary was a Catholic and intended to remain so. If she could have had her own way she would probably have tried to make all her subjects Catholic too. But she knew that this was not possible. So, soon after her return she issued a proclamation saying that no changes were to be made in religion at the moment, but that she and her courtiers were to be allowed to worship as Catholics in peace.

Most people, including Lord James and Lethington, seemed quite content with this arrangement, but not those who were extreme Protestants, like John Knox. He distrusted Mary from the moment she landed at Leith. In St Giles's, the high kirk of Edinburgh, Knox could speak out from his pulpit against her. In sermon after sermon he thundered out against the saying of mass down at Holyroodhouse. To Knox, 'one mass was more fearful than if ten thousand armed enemies were landed in any part of the realm to suppress the holy (Protestant) religion'. He and Mary met four times but they could never agree. Knox looked on Mary as his chief enemy. He was sure she was plotting with the Pope and other Catholic rulers to make Scotland Catholic again, while she looked on him as an outspoken and disobedient subject.

Actually, Mary helped the new Kirk quite a lot. For example, she turned down an offer of help from the Catholic Earl of Huntly to make the country Catholic again by force. When the Pope summoned Catholic Church leaders to attend his Council at Trent in northern Italy to discuss ways of reform-ing the Church, she did nothing to help Scottish bishops to attend. And although she often wrote to tell the Pope how loyal a Catholic she was, she did very little to make Scotland Catholic again.

Mary helped the Kirk in an even more practical way. It was she and her advisers who thought up a plan to make sure that ministers were paid their stipends and that the work of the Kirk was carried on. The Church had lost about two-thirds of its wealth and it would have been impossible for any ruler to recover all of it. Most of it now belonged to the lairds and nobles. So Mary allowed them to hold on to their Church lands. But she arranged for the government to collect the remaining third, keep part of it for its own expenses and leave the rest for the Kirk. In 1562 this third came to £72,000, out of which had to come the cost of collecting it. This left £53,000, and the government gave the Kirk £26,250. The rest was kept by the government, which meant that the Queen did not have to levy taxes for several years.

But John Knox and the other ministers were bitterly disappointed. The sum of money set aside for the Kirk by the government each year was not fixed, and every year the government took more and more and left the Kirk to go short. Knox described this way of sharing out Church property as 'two-thirds freely given to the devil and the third divided between God and the devil'. Can you see what he meant?

For the first three years of her reign Mary was fairly successful in ruling Scotland. Properly guided, she showed that she could be an effective ruler. She made it clear that the law must be obeyed and she did not try to upset the new reformed Kirk. This pleased many of her subjects. At the same time, she disappointed her Catholic subjects and the extreme Protestants were still against her because she herself was still a Catholic.

MARY AND ELIZABETH OF ENGLAND

No matter how successful Mary was at ruling Scotland she also had to get on well with Elizabeth of England who could be dangerous as an enemy. But the Treaty of Edinburgh stood in the way. Mary did not want to sign the Treaty because it would mean giving up her claim to the English throne. Mary's advisers wanted her to sign it. Eventually she agreed to sign and give up the claim if Elizabeth agreed to name Mary as her heir. But Elizabeth did not want to say who her

Mary's shield in 1559 when she was still Dauphine of France. See if you can pick out the English leopards which showed that she claimed to be rightful queen of England as well as queen of Scots

successor should be; as she put it, she did not want 'to hang a *winding-sheet* before her eyes'. In other words, she did not want to name Mary her successor in case Elizabeth's enemies then tried to murder her, to make Mary Queen. So Mary never signed the Treaty of Edinburgh and kept up her claim to be the rightful Queen of England.

For a time there was talk of a meeting between Mary and Elizabeth. Arrangements were made for them to meet at Nottingham in September 1563 but Elizabeth found an excuse for not going. No one knows for sure why Elizabeth did not want to see Mary. They wrote many letters to one another and exchanged presents. For example, Elizabeth sent Mary a ring and Mary gave Elizabeth a large diamond. Once, after she had just had smallpox, Elizabeth wanted to know how Mary had kept her skin unmarked when Mary had had smallpox as a child. Elizabeth was always curious to find out what Mary was like.

Unlike Elizabeth, Mary had been married once and wanted to marry again. But whom was she to marry? It was very important for the country that she made the right choice because her husband would rule alongside her as king. She could not marry one of her own nobles because it would make others jealous and stir up civil war. If she married a foreign prince she would make enemies in other countries because a Protestant husband would offend the Catholics and a Catholic would displease Elizabeth of England as well as her own Protestant subjects. No matter whom she married she was sure to upset somebody.

Elizabeth took a great interest in all Mary's marriage plans. It was she who arranged for the arrival in Scotland of the young Lord Darnley, son of the Scottish Earl of Lennox, one of those nobles who had been banished from Scotland at the time of 'the Rough Wooing'. In 1564 the Earl of Lennox was allowed to return to Scotland. Early in the next year Lord Darnley joined his father.

Opposite: *Henry, Lord Darnley, aged seventeen, with his younger brother, aged six*

Even before he arrived people were talking about Darnley as a possible husband for Mary. As you can see from the family tree on page 8 Mary and Darnley were cousins. They had both the same grandmother, Margaret Tudor, that sister of Henry VIII of England who had married the Earl of Douglas after the death of James IV. Next to Mary, Darnley had the best claim to the English throne. He had been brought up as a Catholic but he had attended Protestant services.

Although Mary had met Darnley earlier in France she had not paid much attention to him. Now he was nearly nineteen years old and very handsome, with golden hair and an oval face. What Mary probably liked most about him was his great height. Mary herself was very tall, but Darnley was even taller, over 2 metres. Soon Mary was describing him as 'the *lustiest* and best *proportioned* long man' that she had seen. When he fell ill with measles at Stirling Castle, Mary nursed him herself night and day. She had fallen headlong in love with Darnley and now determined to marry him.

Everybody disapproved of Darnley as a husband for the Queen. Lord James, now known as the Earl of Moray, disliked him because he would take his place as the Queen's chief adviser. Lethington was against the marriage because it was sure to upset Queen Elizabeth who did not want to see Mary married to another Catholic heir to the English throne. John Knox was afraid that if Mary married another Catholic she would openly try to turn Scotland into a Catholic country again. But Mary still went ahead with preparations for her marriage. She had to get permission from the Pope because she and Darnley were so closely related, but even before the permission came the wedding had taken place early in the morning of Sunday, 29 July 1565 in Holyrood Abbey.

7 *Mary's Reign in Scotland: the Years of Misfortune*

At first, Mary's marriage made her very happy. She and Darnley seemed to be so well matched. To show how much she trusted him she announced that he was to be known as King Henry and that both of them would sign all official papers. But nobles could not stand his swaggering and bullying ways. The Earl of Moray had no respect for him at all. Within a few days of Mary's wedding he rallied his followers at Ayr and marched on Edinburgh, claiming that Mary intended to upset the religious settlement by trying to make Scotland Catholic again.

Mary acted coolly and swiftly to this challenge to her authority. She ordered her followers to muster at Falkirk, Stirling and Kirkintilloch and rode out to join them, taking Darnley with her to give her confidence. Moray entered

A Scottish coin, known as a ryal, that was issued in 1565 to mark Queen Mary's marriage to Lord Darnley. One side shows the queen's shield with the crown and the lion, and with the words, in Latin, 'Whom God has joined together let no man separate'. The other side shows Mary facing her husband, with the Latin words for 'Henry and Mary, by the Grace of God, King and Queen of Scots'

Edinburgh but found nobody to support him. Most people thought that he was only out to win back the power he had lost as a result of Mary's marriage. As soon as he heard that Mary was returning with an army five times bigger than his, he retreated to Dumfries. Here he waited for the help that Elizabeth of England had promised to send him. In the meantime Mary went about rallying support and raising money to pay her soldiers, *pledging* her jewels and writing for help to the King of Spain.

At Dumfries Moray waited in vain for help from England. Elizabeth never liked people to know that she gave help to rebels, especially when they were unsuccessful ones like Moray and his friends. So, when Mary marched south with an army he fled across the Border to Carlisle. Mary had therefore chased her enemies out of Scotland, which is why this rebellion by Moray is known as the Chaseabout Raid.

MURDER AT HOLYROODHOUSE

You can imagine how triumphant Mary felt now. With her husband to help her she had routed her enemies. By early November courtiers knew that she was expecting a baby. This made her more confident still. Soon, she thought, she would have an heir to rule Scotland after her. But she should not have been so confident. Though Elizabeth had not given Moray any help she was still plotting against Mary. Having made enemies of Moray and other Protestant lords, Mary now had to rely on support from her Catholic friends. But they did not have many followers. Besides, the more she depended on them, the more she would alarm the Protestants. Worst of all, she soon discovered what a worthless husband Darnley was. He was more interested in going hunting and drinking with his foolish friends and spending his time with other women than in helping Mary to govern the country. He sulked because he had not been crowned king. The less he did, the less Mary gave him to do. Instead she took advice on how to rule the country from some of her courtiers.

 One of these courtiers was an Italian, David Riccio, who

had come to Scotland in 1561. He was a servant of the ambassador of the Duke of Savoy. He was a fine musician, and, as the Queen loved music, this is how she came to notice him. Soon he was singing bass in her group of court musicians. By 1564 he was one of her private secretaries and dealt with many important matters of state. So powerful did he become, that if anyone at court wanted to speak to the Queen they had to ask him first.

An engraving of Queen Mary's Italian secretary, David Riccio, shown playing his lute

Riccio was a small, dark man, but so full of his own importance that people at court called him '*Seigneur* Davie'. Nobles hated him because he was a foreigner as well as a commoner, and yet he had so much power over them. John Knox was sure that he had been sent to Scotland as a secret agent of the Pope to work for the downfall of the Protestant religion.

It was not long before Mary's enemies saw how they could use Riccio in their plots against her. They told Darnley that 69

Riccio and Mary were lovers. As they expected, Darnley
became so jealous that he joined them in their plot to kill
Riccio. Mary's enemies also promised to crown Darnley king
and make him ruler of Scotland in her place. Because some
of them were facing trial for their part in the Chaseabout
Raid, Darnley promised, in return, to see that the trial was
dropped.

On Saturday, 9 March 1566, three days before the trial
was due to start, Mary's enemies secretly surrounded the
Palace of Holyroodhouse. Upstairs in a small candle-lit room
the Queen was having supper as usual with a few close friends,
including Riccio. Unexpectedly, Darnley joined them. He
accused his wife of being unfaithful. An argument started.
All of a sudden strange noises could be heard in the private
stair outside. The door burst open and there in the doorway
stood one of the *conspirators*, Lord Ruthven, a suit of armour
showing under his cloak. He demanded that the Queen send
Riccio outside. The Queen refused and ordered Ruthven to
leave. Just then other conspirators swarmed into the room.
They seized Riccio, who was cowering behind the Queen and
clinging to her skirts in terror. Grabbing Darnley's dagger,
one of the plotters lunged forward and buried it in Riccio's
side. Then all was in confusion. There were screams and shouts.
Chairs and table were overturned and candles swept away.
Someone brought a light. There in the glow stood the Queen
with a pistol pointed at her stomach, while the wounded
Riccio, kicking, shrieking and begging for mercy, was dragged
outside and hacked to death. Later, more than fifty wounds
were counted on the little Italian's body which had been
carelessly thrown to the foot of the stairs.

THE KIRK O' FIELD MYSTERY

Afterwards when Mary was told that Riccio was dead, she is
reported to have said: 'No more tears; I will think upon a
revenge.' In the meantime she was powerless, a prisoner in
her own palace. The Earl of Moray returned from England

 and Darnley duly kept his side of the bargain by calling off the trial of those who had taken part in the Chaseabout Raid.

Mary waited. Within two days she had won over Darnley, who told her all about the plot. She persuaded him to try to escape with her. Thanks to some friendly guards they were able to slip out of the Palace just after midnight. Soon they were riding almost without stopping down the coast to the castle of Dunbar. There they were joined by some loyal nobles. Within a few days Mary was riding back to Edinburgh with an army of 8,000 men, while her enemies fled to England.

Mary followed up her victory by skilfully turning her enemies against each other. She ordered the murderers of Riccio to be brought to trial, but she forgave Moray and some of his friends, and even allowed them back again into her government. But she could never forgive Darnley for his part in the murder. She could never forget that he had taken part in a plot, to kill not only Riccio, but also herself and their unborn child. Until now she had only despised her husband, now she loathed him,

Not even the birth of a baby son, James, at Edinburgh Castle in June 1566 could bring Mary and Darnley together. He still treated her badly and neglected his duties as king. So she turned for help and advice to one of her nobles, James Hepburn, Earl of Bothwell. He was one of the most powerful nobles in Scotland, with lands scattered over the southern counties. His family prided itself on its loyalty to the royal family. At that time most Scottish nobles took bribes from England but he accepted none. Also, unlike most nobles in Scotland, Bothwell was well educated and had travelled much in England, France and Norway. He had led an adventurous life. At this time he was just over thirty, about 1.6 metres tall and with a *swarthy* complexion. One writer of the time described him as looking like 'an ape in purple'. Many women, however, found him very attractive. Other noblemen distrusted him for his ruthless ambition. They believed that he was out for nothing less than control of Scotland.

With a weak fool for a husband Mary valued Bothwell for his loyalty and strength. He meant so much to her that, when he lay wounded in his castle at Hermitage in October 1566, she rode 30 kilometres over rough country in one day simply to see him. Already, some historians have said, Mary was secretly in love with him. Others disagree and say that Mary was interested in Bothwell only as an adviser.

Mary's third husband, James Hepburn, Earl of Bothwell

Throughout the autumn of 1566 Mary made no secret of her wish to be rid of Darnley. But how was it to be done? If she divorced him she might make her son illegitimate, and this would mean that he might not become King after her death. At Craigmillar Castle, near Edinburgh, Bothwell and some other nobles offered her a way out of her difficulties. They promised to help her, assuring her that she would 'see nothing but good' and that whatever they did Parliament would approve. In return, Mary was to pardon the murderers of Riccio.

72   At the end of the year Mary and her courtiers gathered at

Stirling for the christening of little Prince James. As part of the festivities Mary pardoned Riccio's murderers. Darnley played little part in the celebrations, and did not even turn up for his son's christening. Just after Christmas he left Stirling for Glasgow, near his father's lands in the Lennox district. On the way it was reported that 'he fell deadly sick' of an infectious disease referred to as 'the pox'. About a month later Mary went to visit her husband at Glasgow. Perhaps she was really sorry for him, perhaps she was afraid that he was plotting against her. No one knows. Whatever the reason for her visit, she brought him back with her to Edinburgh to get better again.

Darnley chose to live in an old house, known as Kirk o' Field, standing not far from the Palace on some high ground just outside the town wall. Mary often went to visit him and twice spent the night there. She intended to sleep once more at Kirk o' Field on Sunday, 9 February 1567, the night before Darnley was due to come home to the Palace. At the last minute, however, she remembered that she had promised to attend the wedding of one of her favourite courtiers, and so about ten o'clock she went back to Holyroodhouse.

Early next morning the people of Edinburgh were wakened by a terrible explosion. Coming out to see what had happened, they found Kirk o' Field blown up. In the garden of the house lay the naked body of Darnley, with the corpse of his manservant lying nearby. There was not any trace of the explosion on either of the bodies, but both had been strangled.

Who blew up Kirk o' Field? Was it the same person who murdered Lord Darnley? Did Mary have anything to do with what happened? Had she lured her husband to his death? These are only some of the many questions that people have asked about the mystery of Kirk o' Field. Historians still argue about answers to these questions. Some say that Darnley was the victim of his own plot to murder the Queen. Others think that there was a plot to blow up both Mary and Darnley. Still others believe that there were several plots to murder Darnley and that they somehow got mixed up. So, whoever

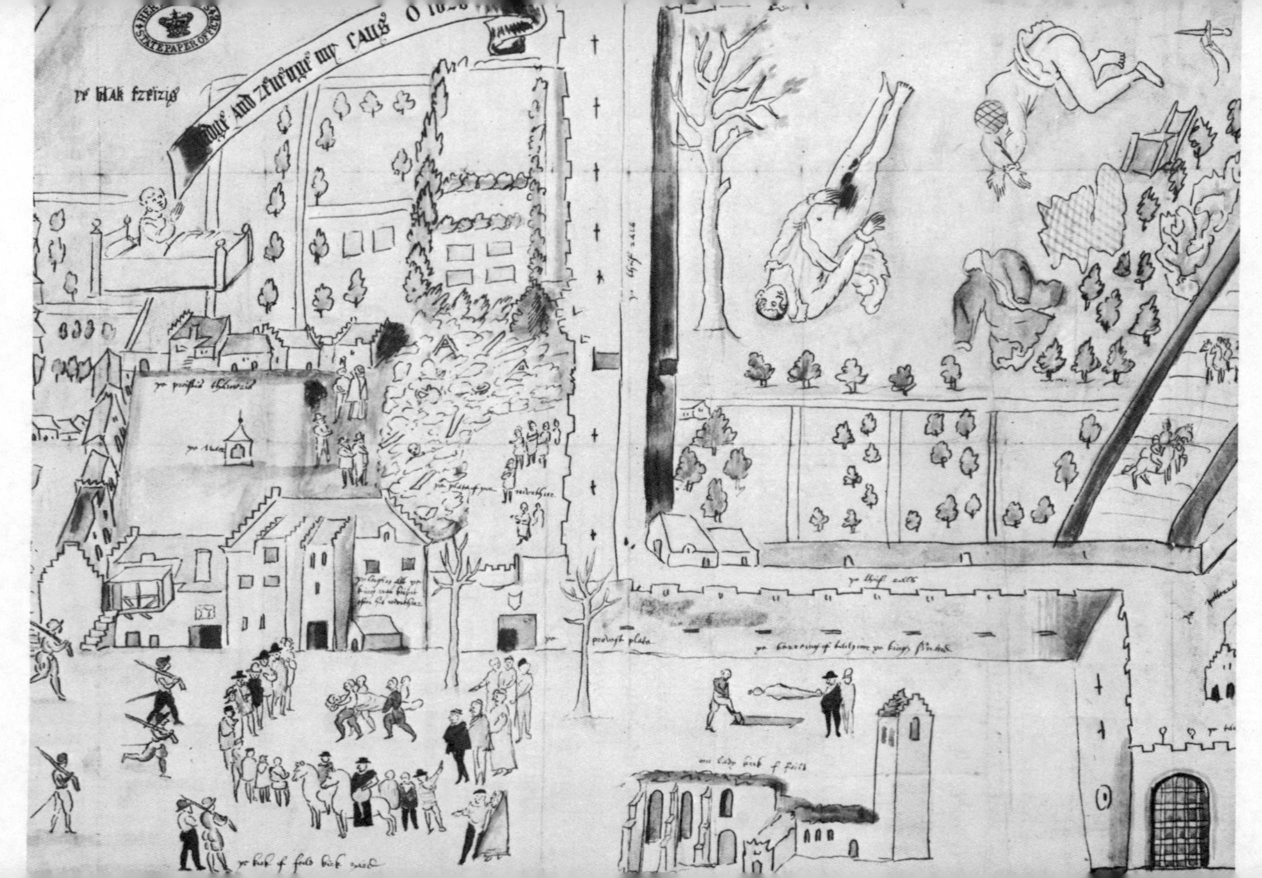
ye blak fzrizis
ye parish churuzid
ou lady kirk of fails
ye kirk of fails kirk zard
prouoyst plate
STATE PAPER OFFICE

blew up Kirk o' Field may not have been the same person who killed Darnley. But we shall never know for certain what happened that night: many of the witnesses either told deliberate lies or were forced to say things under torture which were simply not true.

ANOTHER FATEFUL MARRIAGE

Darnley had many enemies, but the person whom everyone blamed for the murder was the Queen's right-hand man, the Earl of Bothwell. He had been in town at the time and was ruthless enough to kill. Unsigned posters soon appeared all over Edinburgh naming him as the murderer. Then people began to say that the Queen herself might have been involved in the murder. When she promoted him to an important position in the government they said that Bothwell and she had planned the murder together. She made no attempt to bring him to trial: this was left to Darnley's father, the Earl of Lennox. And when the trial did take place, Edinburgh was so full of Bothwell's men that the jury were afraid of them and had to find him not guilty.

People now said that the Queen intended to marry Bothwell. About the end of April 1567, when she was on her way back from visiting her little son at Stirling, she was suddenly stopped near Edinburgh by a body of armed men with Bothwell at their head. They carried the Queen off to his castle at Dunbar. Was all this part of a plan or did Mary go off with Bothwell against her will? Again no one knows; we can only guess. We do know that when she later got the chance to escape she did not take it. At the time people were quite sure that Mary wanted to be captured by Bothwell.

One startling event followed another that year of 1567. In May Bothwell was speedily divorced by his wife and within

Opposite: Look carefully at this rough sketch of the murder of Lord Darnley at Kirk o' Field, Edinburgh. Pick out the remains of the house, the city wall, the bodies of Darnley and his servant, with a dagger, a chair and Darnley's dressing-gown, and Darnley's baby son in his cot with the words 'Judge and Avenge my Cause, O Lord'. What do you think is happening in the foreground?

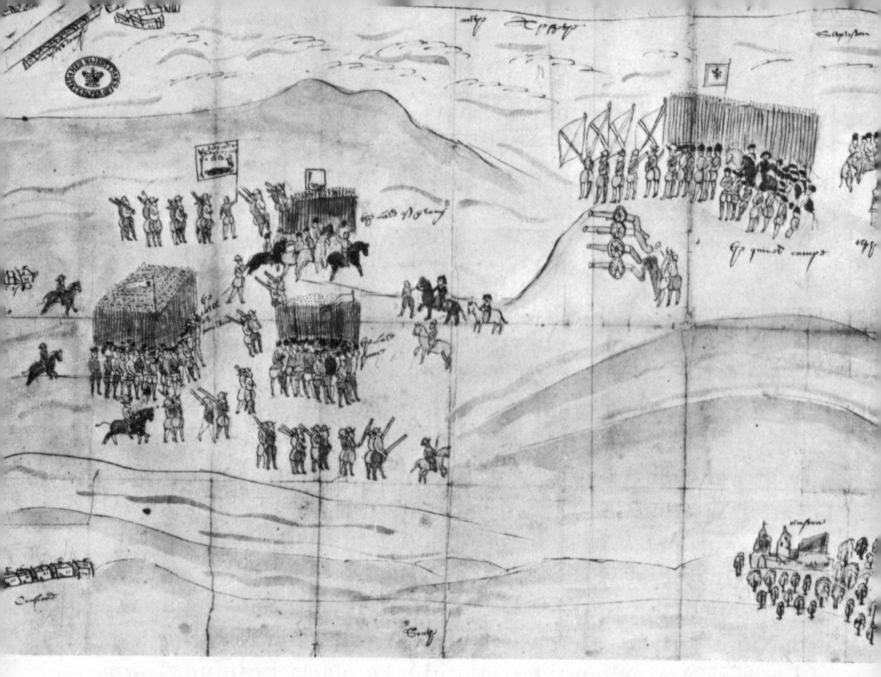

A drawing showing the two armies that met at Carberry Hill near Musselburgh in June 1567. The queen's army is on the right, flying Scottish flags and the royal standard. The rebel lords with their army are on the left. Which army appears the larger? Which seems to have the greater guns? Mary is shown being escorted over to the lords while soldiers from her army ride away to the right

less than a fortnight Mary and he were married at Holyrood. Why did Mary marry Bothwell? Was it out of love or did she marry him simply to make sure of his support in ruling the country? Once again, historians cannot agree on answers to these questions. One thing is certain, Mary's third marriage brought her no happiness. By marrying the man who was suspected of murdering Lord Darnley she lost all chance of making a success of her reign. Now not even the Pope would have anything to do with her, especially since Bothwell was a Protestant. All Mary's enemies said she had done wrong, many of them because they were jealous of the power Bothwell now had.

In June, led by the Earl of Moray, the nobles raised an army and said that they wanted to free Mary from Bothwell's power and avenge the death of Lord Darnley. Mary and Bothwell rode out from Dunbar to meet them, but their army was much smaller than Moray's. On a scorching day the two sides faced each other at Carberry Hill, near Musselburgh. But there was no fighting. Mary's army was short of food and drink and the men simply drifted away. Seeing that their cause was hopeless, Bothwell rode off to try to raise another army, while Mary gave herself up to the nobles. This was the last that Mary and Bothwell ever saw of each other. Deserted and humiliated, Mary was led back to Edinburgh a prisoner to be put up at a house in the High Street. Where they used to cheer her as she passed, the crowds now mocked her and called her the most horrible names.

LOCHLEVEN AND LANGSIDE
Mary was now in the hands of her enemies. Next day she was taken down to Leith and ferried over the water to Fife. She was imprisoned in a gloomy castle on an island in Lochleven. For the next fortnight she was so exhausted she could hardly eat or drink.

Meanwhile, the victorious nobles had to decide what to do with their Queen. They wanted her to divorce Bothwell, but she refused. So they forced her to *abdicate*. They made her son, now aged thirteen months, king in her place as James VI, with the Earl of Moray as regent. At the end of July the little King was solemnly crowned in the parish church of Stirling, with John Knox preaching the sermon. Throughout the country there was great rejoicing: in Edinburgh a thousand bonfires were lit and twenty cannon roared out a salute to the new King.

In her castle prison Mary would know nothing of these celebrations. But now that she had given up her throne she might have expected to have been allowed more freedom. Instead she was watched over more closely than ever as the nobles were scared that someone might try to free her. There seemed little chance of that: Mary's friends outside were too weak and frightened. Bothwell, having failed to raise an army, had fled to Orkney and Shetland where he led the life of a pirate, and had finally sailed away to Norway. Within the Castle of Lochleven, however, there was someone who planned for Mary's escape. He was George Douglas, the brother of her jailer. His first attempt at getting her out failed. As she was being rowed across the Loch dressed as a washerwoman, Mary gave herself away with her slim, pale hands.

Douglas's second attempt was more successful. Mary had also won over a young page in the Castle, named Willie Douglas. On Sunday, 2 May 1568, while serving his master's supper, he deftly picked up the castle keys with his napkin. The Queen and her maidservant were waiting, dressed as countrywomen. All three casually walked out of the Castle, locked the gates behind them and dropped the keys in passing into a cannon. A boat was waiting. With the Queen tucked under the seat, Willie Douglas rowed the boat ashore. There was George Douglas waiting with the laird of Lochleven's best horses. Accompanied only by Willie Douglas, Mary rode off. Two miles on they were joined by Lord Seton, one of her most devoted followers, who took her across the Forth to his castle of Niddry, not far from Queensferry. After ten and a half months as a prisoner Mary slept her first night in freedom.

She had no time to delay, however. Next morning she was off again, riding fast to Hamilton, where members of the Hamilton family were ready to help her. Within a few days many powerful people, including nine earls, seventeen lords, nine bishops and ninety lairds, had signed a bond, pledging themselves to fight for her. Soon she had mustered an army of between 5,000 and 6,000 men. This shows how popular Mary still was.

At the head of her army Mary rode towards Dumbarton, a strong fortress on the Clyde which she hoped to use as her base for winning back her kingdom. The Regent Moray, however, had heard of her escape. He barred her way with an army at Glasgow. On 13 May the two armies met south of

 Glasgow at the village of Langside. Though the Queen's

army was much bigger than the Regent's, it was badly led by the Earl of Argyll. Moray was his brother-in-law, and either Argyll did not want to fight against him or else he had a badly timed attack of *epilepsy*. So, from a nearby hill, Mary had to watch with dismay while her army was mown down by fire from Moray's hagbutters and then scattered by his pikemen. The battle was over in an hour. Mary had to be held back from riding down and rallying on her men herself, but finally she was persuaded to turn horse and flee for safety.

Guided by another loyal supporter, Lord Herries, she rode south over wild and trackless country towards Dumfries. Here, in the south-west, she hoped that many of the Catholic nobles and lairds might come to her aid. But Mary did not find the help she had hoped for. What was she to do now?

If you had been one of her friends there are different things you might have advised her to do. She could raise another army: remember how popular she had been before the battle at Langside; many of the lords who had fought there might be willing to fight for her again. She could leave Scotland and go to France, where she had many friends to look after her. There she could lead a peaceful life away from all the worries of ruling Scotland.

Mary would have turned down both these suggestions. Her mind was made up. She would leave Scotland, not for France but for England. She was a gambler, remember, and perhaps she thought that Elizabeth might be persuaded to help her regain her throne. Whatever her reasons, she rode down to the Solway shore and at three o'clock in the afternoon on Sunday, 16 May 1568, she sailed out in a small fishing-boat. Four hours later she had arrived in England. It was only just under seven years since she had come back to Scotland from France.

8   *Long Years of Captivity*

Mary's sudden arrival in England took everybody by surprise. It was the last thing Elizabeth expected or wanted. Mary was taken to the castle at Carlisle, where the warden treated her with great respect, but wondered what he was to do with her. Elizabeth did not know either. Think how awkward it must have been for her. What would you have advised her to do with Mary? Allow her to stay in England as an honoured guest? Think how dangerous this would have been for Elizabeth: English Catholics might have tried to make Mary Queen in her place. Or should Elizabeth have welcomed Mary and then sent her back to Scotland with an English army to restore her to power again? Wouldn't this have annoyed Elizabeth's Protestant subjects and also involved England in a war she could ill afford?

Elizabeth could not make up her mind what to do with Mary. Probably she would have liked to send Mary back to Scotland, but did not want to upset her ally, the Protestant Regent Moray. Elizabeth's advisers, however, were quite sure that Mary was too much of a threat to England's security to let her go free. The sooner she was safely locked up the better, they said. And in case she tried to slip back over the Border she should be brought farther south. So Mary was taken to the castle of Bolton in the wilds of North Yorkshire, far away from any town.

The English government now had time to decide what to do next. They set up a *commission* to look into Mary's quarrel with her nobles. It met at York and heard arguments from both sides. Mary had advisers who spoke on her behalf. They said that her subjects had rebelled against her and that Elizabeth should give her help to put them down. Moray, speaking for the nobles, said that Mary had been put off the throne because she was not fit to rule. Before long the enquiry turned into a sort of trial, with Mary having to defend herself against Moray and his friends in front of English judges.

During the enquiry Moray and his friends produced a mysterious silver casket. They said this had been taken from one of Bothwell's servants. It contained a collection of papers including some love letters that appeared to have been written between Mary and Bothwell before the death of Darnley. These Casket Letters, as they are called, were meant to prove that Mary and Bothwell had planned Darnley's murder. For centuries historians have argued whether the Casket Letters were false or genuine. Nowadays many think that they were false and were made up of parts of letters written by Mary and Bothwell to other people. If so we shall never know who made them up because the original letters disappeared a long time ago. We only have copies of the letters, which makes it impossible to check the original handwriting. At the time, Elizabeth and her advisers did not think the letters were very important. The enquiry was therefore closed with neither side satisfied. Moray went back to Scotland but Mary remained in England, held prisoner not because of any crime she had committed but because Elizabeth could not think of anything else to do with her.

Thus began Mary's long years of captivity, spent in various English castles. From Bolton she was moved early in 1569 to Tutbury in Staffordshire. It was a bleak place, nearly in ruins and overlooking a marsh. The dampness gave Mary terrible colds and rheumatism. Her jailer was the Earl of Shrewsbury, a fussy but kindly sort of man. Unfortunately, he was completely under the thumb of his wife, Elizabeth, a grim, hard-faced woman who showed Mary very little sympathy.

On the whole, Mary was not treated badly in prison. At first she was allowed to have visitors, although they were carefully watched in case they tried to help her to escape. 81

She had her own courtiers beside her and servants to look after her. These included the faithful George and Willie Douglas from Lochleven, as well as her old friend Mary Seton, the only one of the 'Four Maries' who did not get married. Altogether, there were over thirty people in attendance on her, all paid out of the money that she got from her lands in France.

Mary passed her days in prison as best she could. Tirelessly she embroidered cushion-covers, tapestries and bed-hangings with *monograms* and all kinds of birds, beasts and plants. For exercise she was allowed to go out hunting. She was even allowed to go to the mineral baths at Buxton for the sake of her health. She looked forward to these visits to a town because she was able to meet people. Then Elizabeth got to hear of it and these outings were stopped. Mary wrote many letters to friends and rulers of other countries, but these had often to be smuggled out to avoid the prying eyes of her jailers. She wrote many letters to Elizabeth, begging to be released or at least to see her, but Elizabeth always found an excuse to say no. Once Elizabeth was visiting a house in the district and could easily have arranged a meeting, but the two Queens never met. If they had, can you imagine what they would have said to each other?

The weeks and months of waiting to be set free stretched into years. But supposing Mary had been allowed to go free, where could she have gone? The French did not want her back. And the men who ruled Scotland for her son, James VI, did not want her either. Some people in Scotland wanted her, though mainly because they were against the government. In 1570 the Regent Moray was shot dead in Linlithgow by an enemy. Civil war then broke out in Scotland. The new regent was the Earl of Lennox, grandfather of the young King. His supporters were known as the 'King's Men'. They were helped by soldiers sent up to Scotland by Elizabeth of England. They fought against the 'Queen's Men' those who were still loyal to Queen Mary. Amongst these was Sir William Kirkcaldy of
 Grange, a Fife laird who many people said was the finest

soldier in Scotland. While the rest of Mary's supporters in Scotland had lost heart, as governor of Edinburgh Castle he held out in a siege that lasted more than two years. It was only when the water in the castle well was poisoned, and after English troops with heavy cannon had battered down the castle walls in May 1573, that Kirkcaldy and his men had to surrender. The 'King's Men' gave him no mercy. They hanged him at the mercat cross in Edinburgh and stuck his head on a pole among the ruins of the castle walls. Now Mary's hopes of being restored to Scotland by force were dashed for ever.

CATHOLIC PLOTS

Meanwhile in England many Catholics hoped to free Mary and make her Queen of England in place of Elizabeth. They turned for help to Philip II of Spain who was a powerful Catholic ruler. The Pope, too, was involved in their schemes. In 1570 he *excommunicated* Elizabeth, which meant that Catholics need no longer obey her.

By the 1580s Catholics and Protestants were at each other's throats all over Europe. Laws were made against Catholics in England. In Paris a terrible massacre of *Huguenots* took place in 1572, while in the Netherlands the Protestant Dutch under William the Silent, Prince of Orange, rose in revolt against their Catholic ruler Philip of Spain. Soldiers from England went to help the Dutch. At sea, English sailors raided Spanish treasure ships. War between Protestant England and Catholic Spain seemed unavoidable. You can read more about these events in two other 'Then and There' books, 'The Huguenots' and 'William the Silent and the Dutch Revolt'.

Then in 1584 a Catholic murdered William the Silent. Suppose somebody murdered Queen Elizabeth? People in England were frightened that their country would be torn by civil war and invaded by Spanish troops; the Spaniards would make Mary Queen of England and the hated mass would be said again in English churches. Now more than ever before Protestant Englishmen looked on Catholic Mary with fear and hatred. An Act of Parliament was passed which said that 83 anyone who plotted to kill Elizabeth or who gained from such a plot should be put to death. It was clearly to stamp out plots to put Mary on the throne.

The man who made it his business to see that such a plot did not succeed was Elizabeth's Secretary of State, Sir Francis Walsingham, a man who hated Roman Catholics. To protect the Queen he employed many spies. He knew that Mary was involved in plots against Elizabeth, but did not have enough evidence to prove her guilty. So Walsingham now decided to use his spies to lure Mary into a deadly trap.

Mary had now been Elizabeth's prisoner for seventeen years. At the end of 1585 she was moved from Tutbury Castle to the moated manor house of Chartley nearby. By this time she was in the care of a new jailer, Sir Amyas Paulet, a harsh, cruel man who disliked her intensely. He did everything possible to make life unpleasant for her, not even allowing her to go out for exercise. He also stopped her from receiving any letters, so that Mary felt cut off from the outside world and was desperate to know what was going on. Walsingham persuaded one of Mary's secret agents, Gilbert Gifford, to become one of his spies and act as a double agent. This was their plan: Gifford was to see to it that Mary started up writing letters again to the French ambassador in London. Walsingham would allow the ambassador to pass on letters between Mary and her friends on the continent. Gifford was to make sure that all Mary's letters were opened and read.

Somehow, Gifford had to arrange for Mary's letters to be smuggled out and in. How was he to do it? He found a way by using beer-casks. Chartley had no brew-house, and so beer had to be brought in from the local town of Burton-upon-Trent. Gifford arranged for Mary's letters to be smuggled in the beer-casks. Mary leapt at the chance of getting in touch with her friends again. She wrote her letters, which her secretary put into code, and then wrapped them up in a leather case that was stuffed into the stopper of an empty beer-cask. The brewer took away the empty barrels and handed the packet of letters to Gifford who was supposed to deliver them to the French ambassador. Unknown to Mary, however, Gifford first passed on the letters to Walsingham and his agents, who knew how to read the code. Mary's enemies therefore knew all about what passed in her secret letters.

Among the people who wrote to Mary was Sir Anthony Babington, a rich young Catholic gentleman from Derbyshire, who planned to free her. Walsingham now arranged for Babington and Mary to write to each other. Soon he found out all about Babington's plot. Elizabeth was to be murdered, Mary set free and with foreign help made Queen of England. By the end of July 1586 Walsingham had enough evidence of Mary's guilt. All he had to do was to round up Babington and the other conspirators. Mary knew nothing of all this when one day in August her jailer suddenly said that she could go out hunting. When she saw some horsemen riding across the moors to meet her she thought they might be friends coming to rescue her. Imagine her shock and dismay when they said they had been sent by Elizabeth to arrest her. Mary had fallen right into Walsingham's trap.

TRIAL AND EXECUTION

Mary was taken to Fotheringay, a tall grim castle that seemed to frown over the flat Northamptonshire countryside. Meanwhile, a body of thirty-six lords and judges prepared to bring her to trial. At first Mary refused to have anything to do with such proceedings. She claimed that no court had the right to try a queen, but finally she agreed to appear and defend herself against their charges.

Mary's trial took place in a long room above the great hall of Fotheringay Castle. Nothing like it had ever been seen before in England. Crowds of local people gathered to watch. Imagine that you were one of the spectators. At the far end of the room you would have seen a throne under a high canopy showing the royal arms of England. This was for Queen Elizabeth but she did not attend. It reminded people that this was her court. Opposite the throne was a red velvet chair for Mary. In between stood a long table, piled with papers. Here

sat the lawyers, while on each side of the room sat the lords and judges who would carry out the trial.

It was just after nine o'clock in the morning of 15 October 1586 when the trial began. The noise and chatter of the crowd suddenly died down when Mary came in and took her seat. If this was your first glimpse of the famous Queen of Scots you must have had a big shock. Instead of the dazzling young girl of whose beauty poets had sung, you would see a limping, middle-aged woman, her face pale and puffy, her body bent with rheumatism and plump from lack of exercise.

Yet throughout the trial you could not have helped being impressed by the dignified way Mary behaved. You would have heard the case made out against her and listened to her defence. She denied all the charges of plotting against Queen Elizabeth. Anything she had done, she said, was simply to set herself free from unlawful imprisonment. As was usual at this time in criminal cases, Mary had to conduct her own defence without any help from lawyers. She knew no English law and was not allowed to see any of the documents brought in evidence against her. The trial lasted two days. Then the judges rode off to consult Queen Elizabeth at Westminster.

No one was surprised when Mary was found guilty. It was now up to Elizabeth to pass sentence of death. For nearly three months Elizabeth put off signing the death warrant. Though she knew that as long as Mary lived she was not safe, she hated the idea of putting another queen to death. All the while, members of Parliament made angry speeches urging her to sign. At the same time foreign rulers wrote begging her to be merciful. From Scotland came a feeble protest from James VI, Mary's son, now aged nearly twenty. But Elizabeth knew she need not take his protest seriously: if Elizabeth died, he had a strong claim to her throne. James dared not offend Elizabeth in case she did not name him as her successor. Besides, James had never known his mother and had been brought up by his tutor and guardians to hate her. This is why he did nothing to help her.

At last in January 1587 Elizabeth could put off signing Mary's death warrant no longer. Alarming stories were going about of another plot to murder her, of Mary having escaped, of London being on fire, and of Spanish troops having landed in Wales. It is said that her secretary placed Mary's death warrant under a pile of papers on her desk, and so without looking, Elizabeth signed away Mary's life.

Mary spent her last days quietly, giving away *mementoes* to her loyal friends and servants. In these later years her religion had been a great comfort, so she spent much of her time in prayer. On the day fixed for her execution, Wednesday, 8 February 1587, she rose early and dressed in her best gown of black satin. Calmly she went downstairs to the great hall of the castle where a large crowd had gathered. In the centre a wooden platform had been put up, with the block on it all draped in black, the axe lying near at hand. A royal offical

The executioner is about to bring down his axe in this drawing of the execution of Mary. Her ladies stand weeping on the left. Outside her clothes are being burned.

The white marble effigy of Mary Queen of Scots that her son, James VI and I, put on her tomb in Westminster Abbey. How well do you think James treated his mother?

read out the death warrant, though Mary hardly seemed to hear. The Dean of Peterborough then began to pray according to the Church of England form of service, but Mary prayed to herself in the Catholic way. Carefully the executioners helped her ladies to undress her until she was standing in only a dark red petticoat. She forgave all her enemies and told her friends not to weep for her. Then she lay down with her arms outstretched and her head on the block. With two strokes of his axe the executioner's work was done.

When the news reached Elizabeth, she broke down in tears and fiercely blamed her secretary for making her sign the death warrant. In London people cheered, rang church bells and lit bonfires in the streets. In France there was deep mourning. In Scotland some of Mary's friends threatened to march south and burn down Newcastle, but King James did nothing to avenge his mother's execution. Sixteen years later in 1603 when Elizabeth died he got his reward: he became king of England and so united the two countries. The Kirk and the Protestant religion were now safe. Thus ended the life of Mary Queen of Scots, to some a beautiful she-devil, to others a much-wronged Catholic martyr, to all a woman of the deepest mystery.

How Do We Know?

We shall probably never know what Mary Queen of Scots was really like. People in her lifetime said so many different things about her. This is why novelists and playwrights have found her such a fascinating person to write about. Anybody who reads about Mary has to interpret the source material very carefully. There is no shortage of this. It consists of official documents such as ambassadors' reports, Acts of Parliament, orders to generals, as well as of private papers, including letters, *memoirs* and household accounts. You can read some of the things people wrote about Mary in her own time and later in Ian B. Cowan's 'The *Enigma* of Mary Stewart'. Three modern books about Mary are Antonia Fraser's 'Mary Queen of Scots', Gordon Donaldson's 'Mary Queen of Scots' and 'Mary Queen of Scots, the Fair Devil of Scotland' by Jean Plaidy. This last book is full of beautiful pictures. In all of these books you can see for yourself which sources the authors used.

Most of the books on the Scottish Reformation are rather heavy going. There is a modern biography of John Knox by Jasper Ridley. But it might be better if you looked up entries on Knox as well as Luther and Calvin in encyclopedias, such as the 'Oxford Junior Encyclopedia' and the 'Children's Britannica'. You might like to dip into Knox's own 'History of the Reformation in Scotland', edited by W. Croft Dickinson. This will give you an idea of what the man was like from the way he wrote. Knox wrote mainly in English. You can sample sixteenth-century Scots in Sir David Lindsay's play 'A Satire of the Three Estates' in a modern edition by Matthew McDiarmid. Extracts from both these sources are to be found in 'A Source Book of Scottish History', edited by Dickinson, Donaldson and Milne. Another collection of documents from this time is Agnes Mure Mackenzie's 'Scottish Pageant (1513–1625)'. A visit to the National Portrait Gallery of Scotland in Edinburgh will show you what many of the people in this book looked like.

Things To Do

1. Look out for novels, plays and films about Mary and see whether the story they tell is like what you have read in this book.
2. Draw a strip cartoon showing some of the scenes in Mary's life. Copy pictures of people and places mentioned in this book and make a frieze on the walls of your classroom.
3. Visit places mentioned in this book associated with Mary and the Reformation: for example Linlithgow Palace, the Palace of Holyroodhouse, St Andrews Castle, St Giles' Cathedral.
4. Imagine that you are working for a tourist agency. Make a list of places to be visited on a tour called 'In the Tracks of Mary Queen of Scots'. Copy out a large map and enter on it the names of places associated with Mary's life and times. Illustrate the map with postcards and write a few sentences about each place to say what happened there in Mary's time.
5. Imagine you are living in the days of Mary Stewart. Write one of the following:
   (a) An argument between two Scottish noblemen in the 1540s about whether Scotland should be an ally of France or England.
   (b) A comparison by a servant of Mary Queen of Scots of life at the French court and life in Scotland.
   (c) An interview by John Knox about his life so far and about the kind of Church he would like to see set up in Scotland.
   (d) An explanation by a Roman Catholic telling how and why he tried to free Mary from her English prison.
   (e) An explanation by Queen Elizabeth, in 1587, of her treatment of Mary.
6. Discuss in class:
   (a) That the Reformation in Scotland could have been avoided.
   (b) That Mary was responsible for her own misfortune.
7. Listen to music of the sixteenth century. Here are two records to look out for: 'Musick Fyne – Songs and Dances of the Scottish Court', 33SR 133, and 'A History of Scottish Music 1', SRSS1.
8. Other books in the 'Then and There' series you might like to read are: 'Scotland in the Days of James VI', 'A Reformation Family', 'Elizabethan Court', 'William the Silent and the Dutch Revolt', 'The Huguenots', 'Luther and the Reformation', and 'Spain and her Empire under Philip II'.

Glossary

abbot, head of monks in an abbey
to abdicate, to give up a position, such as being a King or a ruler
to allege, to say
Alliance, arrangement to work together
ambassador, person who is sent by one ruler to speak to another
Apostles, the first twelve followers of Christ
apothecary, old name for chemist
arquebus, old-fashioned hand-gun
audible, able to be heard
backgammon, game for two people played on a board with dice and
    counters
bairns, Scots word for children
banquet, large feast
bishop, churchman in charge of a diocese
blasphemous, showing no respect to God
to blockade, to prevent movement of ships in and out of port
boldened, made bold
bombardment, attack with heavy guns
bursary, money given to a student to pay his fees
canon law, law of the Catholic Church
canopy, overhanging cover
cardinal, high official of the Catholic Church who helps to elect the
    Pope
cassock, gown worn by priest
casting, throwing
cavalry, soldiers on horseback
catechism, list of religious beliefs in form of questions and answers
cathedral, most important church in a diocese
chancellor, chief adviser of a ruler
chaplain, private minister or priest to a particular person or group
châteaux, French for castles
chronicler, one who keeps a chronicle or note of passing events
clergy, churchmen
commendator, layman appointed temporarily to look after abbey or
    diocese
commission, body of people appointed to carry out a special task
commode, piece of furniture which has a lavatory pot inside

concubine, woman who lives with a man and who is not his wife
conspirator, plotter
coronet, small crown
courtier, person who is often at a ruler's court
crooked, bent with age
croquet, game, played on a lawn, in which wooden balls are driven
  with mallets through hoops
damask, thick, smooth linen cloth
damnable, hateful
dauphin, title of the French King's eldest son; his wife was known as
  the Dauphine
deacon, in a presbyterian church one who looks after money matters
defile, make dirty
diocese, area where a bishop is responsible for church matters
disciple, follower
divinity, study of religion
dolour, suffering,
dowered with, with money that comes from a girl's family when she
  marries
dropsy, illness in which the patient's body swells up with fluid
durst, dared
enigma, riddle
epilepsy, a sickness where the patient has fits and falls to the ground
to excommunicate, to cut off from the Church
farthingale, hooped petticoat for filling out a woman's skirts
fleur-de-lys, French for lily, the emblem of the French kings
fresco, painting done on wet plaster
friary, place where friars (humble order of monks) live
galley, low sea-going ship pulled by oars
galliard, lively dance for two
guid, Scots for good
haar, cold sea-fog on the east coast of Scotland or England
hagbutter, soldier armed with an arquebus
heresy, religious belief that is different from the Church's teaching
heretic, person who holds to a heresy
heretofore, until now
hostage, person held by enemies as a guarantee of other's good
  behaviour
Huguenot, French Protestant
idolatrous, worshipping false gods or idols
illegitimate, born to unmarried parents
image, artificial likeness such as a picture or statue
impiety, lack of respect for God, wickedness

to incur, to bring on or cause
to intervene, to come between
ire, anger
kirk, Scots word for church
lamentations, expressions of regret or grief
links, sandy ground near a sea-shore
living, piece of property to support a clergyman
livre, old French coin
loose-living, misbehaviour
Lord Treasurer, member of government in charge of money
Lords of the Congregation, Protestant Lords in Scotland
lustiest, strongest
lute, stringed musical instrument
manifestly, clearly
mantle, loose sleeveless cloak
manuscript, hand-written document
mass, religious ceremony in Catholic Church services in memory of
    Christ's Last Supper
mementoes, gifts by which to remember a person
memoirs, what a person remembers and writes about his own life
mercat cross, Scots for market cross
monastery, place where monks live
monastic, to do with a monastery
monogram, figure made up of two or more letters intertwined
multitude, crowd
notary, person who is allowed to draw up legal contracts
nunnery, place where nuns live
outlays, expenses
pageant, colourful play or show, usually about an event in the past
pamphlet, paperback booklet
paramour, girl friend
pavane, slow, stately dance
pike, long wooden pole with pointed steel or iron end
pilgrimage, journey made by a pilgrim to visit a holy place
pledging, handing over as security for something
pluralism, holding more than one job
pomander, small case for holding perfumed substance
portion, allowance of food for one person
postern gate, side gate of a castle
precincts, grounds especially Church land enclosed by a boundary
presbyterian, to do with a Church ruled by 'presbyters' or elders
prior, chief monk in a priory

priory, small monastery
progeny, children
proportioned, sized and shaped
Provincial Council, chief churchmen in a province of the Catholic
    Church, e.g. Scotland
reek, Scots for smoke
to reform, to make better by removing faults
regent, person who rules while the king or queen is too young to do so
Reformation, movement for reform of Catholic Church
to reimburse, to repay
the Renaissance, revival of interest in Greek and Roman art and
    literature
representative, someone who acts for someone else
revenues, income
revolution, great change
ruby, red jewel
rudiments, first things to be learnt
sable, valuable dark brown fur
to sack, to rob a city
salutations, greetings
sapphire, blue jewel
satire, poem, play or story in which the author makes fun of people
    who are wicked or foolish
seculars, people who are not churchmen
seigneur, French for lord
song-school, school to train choir-boys
sou, old French coin worth a twentieth of a livre
stipend, minister's salary
summons, official call to do something
swarthy, dark
symbol, something standing for something else
testoon, old silver coin
theology, study of religion
thither, there
Three Estates, nobles, clergy and merchants in the Scottish parliament
to wit, that is to say
vestment, robe worn by priest
vicar, churchman responsible for a parish, or standing in for another
virginals, musical instrument like a piano but without legs
virtuous, good
wench, girl
winding-sheet, sheet for wrapping up a corpse

Index